Should I Go to the Teacher?

Should I Go to the Teacher?

Developing a Cooperative Relationship with Your Child's School Community

Susan M. Benjamin

Susan Sanchez

HEINEMANN

Portsmouth, NH

Heinemann
A division of Reed Elsevier Inc.
361 Hanover Street
Portsmouth, NH 03801-3912
Offices and agents throughout the world

Portions of the text originally appeared in Susan Benjamin's columns in *The Newton Graphic* and *THE NEWTON TAB*. Reprinted by permission of the publishers.

Although suggestions for communication are offered, each home school situation is different, and it is ultimately the decision of the family as to how to best communicate with the school.

All names, anecdotes, and scenarios are fictitious, yet may constitute a composite of or be broadly based on actual situations.

Library of Congress Cataloging-in-Publication Data

Benjamin, Susan M.
    Should I go to the teacher? : developing a cooperative
relationship with your child's school community / Susan M. Benjamin,
Susan Sanchez.
      p.   cm.
    ISBN 0-435-08126-8 (alk. paper)
    1. Parent-teacher relationships—United States.   2. Parent-teacher
conferences—United States.   3. Home and school—United States.
I. Sanchez, Susan. II. Title.
LC226.6.B45 1996
370.19′312-dc20   95-31723
                                                CIP

Editor: Cheryl Kimball
Production: Vicki Kasabian
Cover design: Lisa Sawlit
Book design: Jenny Jensen Greenleaf

99 98 97 96 95   DA   1 2 3 4 5 6 7 8 9
Printed in the United States of America on acid-free paper

To Barry,
for the years of support that contributed
to the completion of this work.

Contents

Contents

Contents

Acknowledgments

We are grateful to our many students and their families, as well as to our colleagues and friends, who over the years have enriched our lives as professionals and provided much of the impetus for writing this book.

During the writing process, we reached out to many individuals, who graciously contributed their insights, expertise, and support:

Thanks to *The Newton Graphic* and its editor, Ellen Ishkanian, for granting permission for material to be drawn from Susan Benjamin's previously published newspaper columns.

Thanks to the parents, school administrators, and other professionals who read parts of the manuscript at various stages and offered valuable and valued suggestions: Dr. Mozelle Berkowitz, Dr. Irwin Blumer, Enid Dockser, Ronald Dockser, Dr. Irene Fountas, Ethel Furst, Davida Fox-Melanson, Leo Melanson, Barbara Meyer, Anne Puchkoff, Philip Reddy, Ellen Rosenberg, Arlyn Schneider, Elaine Shooman, Dr. Raymond Shurtleff, Dr. Charles Stiles, Ruthann Stiles, Laurie Swett, and Dr. Alice Axelrod Zimelman.

Thanks to the following people, who were particularly helpful in providing us with background information and other research assistance: Dr. Joseph Adolph, Nancy Adolph, Linda Braun, Susan Brink, Kathleen Carpenter, George Christopher, Audrey Cooper, Barbara Golder, Donna Goldman, Ernestine Hooper, Ruth Hoshino, Donna Johns, Patricia Kelley, Dr. Marcia Krasnow, Myrna Landay, Melva Leiter, Alexander Lelchook, Louise Loewenstein, Howard Monroe, Barbara Morton, Carol Nicolucci, Robin Norman, Patricia

Palmer, Laura Perkins, Jane Ravid, Jane Roderick, Ketty Rosenfeld, Ruth Rubinow, Susan Shamus, Carolyn Shapiro, Dr. Jerome Schultz, Sheila Snyder, *The Newton Tab* staff, Ann Tobojka, Joseph Utka, Donna Verdun, and Lydia Vine.

Thanks to "The Book Group" members Ellen Cone, Karen Mandell, Lesley Perlman, Sharon Sinel, and Roberta Yellen; we appreciate your contributions.

Thanks to Heinemann, and in particular to publisher Cheryl Kimball, production editor Vicki Kasabian, and permissions coordinator Roberta Lew. Their practical, thoughtful suggestions and their encouragement exemplified the spirit of collaboration and will always be remembered.

Thanks to our families for their continuous support: Jerome Katz, who offered his patience and advice, as well as his assurance that it is acceptable to end a sentence with a preposition; our mothers, Thelma Katz Herman and the late Virginia Loose, who encouraged us to "keep working" as we approached our manuscript submission date; Robert and Ezra Benjamin, whose school experiences meant this book could be written from a parent's as well as an educator's perspective; to our husbands, Ricardo, for his patience during long work hours, and Barry, for his willingness to read and react to chapters at any time of day or night, and even give up the use of his desk so the manuscript could be completed.

The purpose of this book is to help children. Children benefit when teachers and families are able to relate well to each other. Our recommendations for how this can be accomplished attempt to remain sensitive to the needs of children, families, and school staff alike. They are broadly based on the Getzels and Guba social systems model, which is a useful way of looking at how individual needs can correspond or conflict with organizational expectations despite common goals. Please remember that these suggestions need to be considered in the context of individual situations; not all of them will be effective all of the time. They are offered as options, with the understanding that we, too, are learners, continually attempting to improve our own communication skills.

—*Susan M. Benjamin and Susan Sanchez*

Introduction

No more pencils, no more books,
no more teacher's dirty looks!

Remember this jingle? It seems to portray teachers as less than supportive. But is this really true? We say no. But channels of communication among parents, teachers, and children can break down. Have you ever found that approaching your child's teacher with a concern made matters more difficult than if you had decided not to get involved? If this has occurred, ineffective communication with the teacher may have interfered with your ability to resolve the situation. On the other hand, if your approach has eased a concern and contributed to finding a successful solution, you have probably communicated effectively. When this is the case, you are likely to maintain a positive and ongoing relationship with the teacher, to handle concerns well, and to provide your child with support. Consider the following situation:

> David came home from school at the usual time, but the expression on his face was different from other days. It was obvious to anyone near him that he was unhappy. The report card in his hand told much of the story. Not only were the grades lower than expected but the anecdotal comments, the ones that the teachers were always telling everyone were so important, indicated disappointment with David's work.
>
> That evening, David's father, greatly disturbed by the report card, said to David, "I thought you were a good student." The father then asked, "Why didn't your teacher let me know you were having problems?" David said nothing.

Because the father had unanswered questions, he decided to find out what had happened. During his lunch hour, he called David's school to speak with the teacher. A kind but firm secretary said, "The teacher can't talk to you now, but I will ask her to return your call."

The teacher called back later in the day but said she could only speak for a minute because her class was waiting for her. The teacher, however, did say, "But I sent you a note!"

With little opportunity to respond, David's father was told by the teacher that she could meet with him in two weeks. Thinking this was too long to wait, David's father, now confused and annoyed, responded, "It seems that you're putting me off. I can't wait that long. I'm going to take this to the principal!"

Feeling threatened, concerned about the phone call, and worried about what the principal might think, the teacher spoke to the principal regarding the situation.

For David's father, frustration had now become anger. Later that afternoon he called the principal.

This scenario illustrates what can happen when the goal of helping your child succeed is thwarted by well intended but misdirected behavior. This can cause all involved to experience the "quicksand effect." When one negative reaction leads to another, new problems can be created, just as each attempt to pull oneself out of quicksand can result in everyone being sucked in a little deeper.

If you notice a situation is escalating, stop to think about what is actually happening. Are things becoming more complicated than necessary or are your responses justified? Think about the following questions:

Did the father act appropriately?

Did the teacher act appropriately?

Could either have handled things differently?

To what extent did the father communicate with his son before contacting the school?

Was the father correct to go to the principal?

Will the issues be resolved?

Will this experience affect future relationships?

When you read or hear about things that happen to someone else, it is often easier to analyze what you would support or question than if they were happening to you. When you are emotionally involved, making good decisions can be difficult. What is clear in this scenario is that incorrect assumptions, missed signals, and ineffective communication caused things to build up and get out of hand.

Your first responsibility is to your child. This book will help you serve your child well by suggesting ways to work to maintain good relationships with teachers and other school staff members, both when you have concerns and when things are going smoothly.

Chapter 1

But I Communicate Just Fine!

The Importance of Developing Effective Communication Skills

"What did Katie do *this* time?"

"What's the point of homework if *I* have to do it every night?"

"That teacher just won't give Alex a chance!"

"How will I ever get to the school play tonight?"

"I wonder how Richard is doing in math?"

Struggling with busy schedules, it's easy to become frustrated planning for your work, volunteer activities, after-school care, family time, and children's school needs. As a parent of an elementary school–aged child, these concerns probably sound familiar.

Now that you've met the challenges of your child's infancy and early childhood, you have a new set of demands to become involved at school, to understand how the school operates, and to establish a working relationship with a new teacher or teachers every year. While your goal right now may only be getting through each day, keep in mind the familiar advice of other parents to "enjoy this time. It goes quickly." Remember also that as your child gets older, your involvement at school will change. You want to look back at your child's elementary school days with rich memories rather than missed opportunities or regrets.

One of the ways you can successfully meet these challenges is by developing and using good communication skills with your child's teachers. Acquiring these skills will help you avoid common mistakes, increase sensitivity to the needs of others, and build trust between you and the teacher. Even if your child has not had significant problems in the classroom, you will learn how to avoid many difficulties before they occur. By making an effort to see the point of view of school personnel, and the *value* in seeing it, you will be empowering yourself to prevent misunderstandings at school.

In order to enable your communication with school to be effective, it may be helpful first to take a closer look at your needs and concerns and the demands on your time.

Notices from School

Elementary school children may take home several notices from school per week. If the notices are not left at school, food-stained beyond recognition, or lost in a pile of other papers to deal with later, many will eventually be sent back to school with a response such as a signature, money, or both.

These notices represent the tip of the iceberg regarding communication between home and school. The school knows that sending notices home not only keeps the school running smoothly but provides a vital link between you and the school. However, your objective with school notices may be similar to that of many families; do only what you must, mark necessary dates on the calendar, and keep the stack as small as possible.

Communications from school inform you, invite you, and include you in your child's education. Informational notices, such as those explaining classroom expectations or policies, require only that you read them. Others require you to respond only if interested, such as announcements in a regular classroom or school newsletter, which will often be packed full of information. One parent noted, "It's hard to keep track. There is so much going on." Still other notices ask you to *do* something. They may request your participation at a PTO committee meeting, a parent-teacher conference, or on a community-wide advisory board.

All these communications represent an even broader challenge: juggling your own busy life with your child's (or, even more

2

challenging, your children's) school career. The schools are not looking for your involvement just to complicate your lives and add to your stress. They believe that in the long run your participation will help your child achieve better.

Look Back Before You Look Ahead

Although you may be used to sending your children off to daycare or preschool, school communications may be different when your children enter kindergarten. The whole family will undergo a new transition and will have an opportunity to regroup. While children do their job of learning, you too, are entering a process of determining how you can best support them.

How do you know what's right? Begin by looking at your own life experiences and your current family situation. This often dictates your behavior and sets the tone for the manner in which you communicate. Consider the examples set by your own parents. Did they make their expectations clear? Were they involved or uninvolved? How supportive were they? How did they demonstrate their support?

Perhaps you remember the Cleavers from the television show "Leave It to Beaver." June, the mother, always seemed to have the energy to do things like bake cookies, volunteer for class trips, or attend PTO meetings, while Ward, the father, went off to work. June was clearly a "milk and cookies" mom and was an idealized product of her day.

However, family structures have changed. Although this lifestyle still exists, it can no longer be taken for granted. Your family may more closely resemble the Huxtables in "The Cosby Show." Claire and Cliff Huxtable each have a career and struggle with conflicts that reflect some of the complexities of this generation.

But the Huxtables may not fit your situation, either. Just as extended families often shared responsibility for child care in the past, "milk and cookies" fathers, single parents, stepparents, grandparents, and others continue to play this role today. Regardless of who the caretaker is and despite employers' increasing flexibility in adapting to families' needs, many households have no one at home to greet children when they return from school.

3

Even if your family resembles the Cleaver's, it's likely that you'll be challenged in ways that will cause you to question what to do or whom to contact. If the school is slow in calling you back or your child comes home crying because "The teacher doesn't like me," you, too, can be caught unsure of how to respond.

What Other Aspects of Yourself Do You Bring to Your Child's School?

Just as your life is full, so is your past. Your background and experiences shape your values, beliefs, and attitudes. These elements form the basis of communication with your child's teacher, which will affect your relationship. In sharing expectations with families, teachers must be sensitive to varying communication styles and individual family needs. Perhaps you can identify with the comments of the following parents.

> "Just because it's 'in' to be involved, hanging around school is not for me. You can count on me to return notices and attend the yearly conference, but that's about it."
>
> "I've never been involved in more than a superficial way. I'm not interested in being the teacher's friend."
>
> "My mother never discussed anything about school. It's a different world. We have to get more involved than our parents did."
>
> "I care and my child knows it, even if I don't participate."
>
> "I'm never embarrassed to advocate for my child, and I never feel guilty that I am making waves."

Are you among those parents who are intimidated by schools? Do you feel out of place or uncomfortable as soon as you walk through the front door of a school? Just as a medicinal odor triggers anxiety and a sinking sensation for some upon entering a hospital, you may be affected by the feel of a school. When you visit a school, you may be struck by what appears to be a deserted corridor, despite background noise that tells you much is happening.

As you enter a classroom, the scaled-down furnishings are hard to ignore. One parent noted, "I had forgotten how small everything was. It reminded me of when I was in school." Your experiences as a student may come to mind as well. Do you remember the time you got into trouble and your family never found out? One parent recalls, "The teacher kicked me out of the classroom because I was talking in class." As an adult, this parent still remembers the terror she felt standing in the corridor, worrying about whether the principal would walk by and question why she was there.

Even when you have only positive memories, seeing your child's school and classroom as an adult can cause apprehension. This may occur when you come for a routine conference or for another purpose, as in the following scenario.

> A fifth-grade class was learning to use the scientific method of investigation. The teacher thought, "What a great opportunity to invite Yolanda's mother, a scientist, to come in and talk about the work she does in her laboratory. She doesn't get to school often, yet she indicated a willingness to do something like this early in the fall. This would be terrific for everyone."
>
> After the parent successfully completed the presentation, she confided to the teacher that she had had misgivings about talking to her daughter's class. She said, "It was one thing for me to worry at home about whether I was gearing the presentation to the right level, but when I got into the classroom, I panicked: 'How will I get the children's attention? Where am I supposed to stand? Will I be able to handle a behavior problem?' I was relieved that the class was cooperative and made my job easy."

"The teacher is always right" is a belief you may remember your family expressing when you were a child, and this view of the teacher may still dictate your behavior. It might go against your grain to question the teacher. One mother justifies this attitude by believing it is good for her child to be flexible and conform to what the teacher thinks is best, even if the teacher is wrong or gives an assignment that seems like a waste of time.

Similarly, other parents support this view as a need for children to go through a rite of passage. Often teachers go unchallenged due to deep-seated beliefs that the teacher should not be questioned even when families disagree with the instructional goals.

Interestingly, most teachers *don't* think they are always right and expect to be challenged as long as their professionalism is respected. Consequently, if you attempt to avoid stepping on the teacher's toes, your child may miss out. The parent in the following situation was faced with just such a difficult decision.

A third-grade teacher was known to discipline students by sending them to the office bench for "cooling off" frequently. One parent, worried about what her daughter was missing in the classroom when she frequently had to cool off, cautiously confronted the teacher despite an upbringing that told her not to do this.

When the teacher was questioned, he rethought his behavior and decided that he was establishing a pattern of excluding children from his class that was clearly becoming excessive.

Although confronting the teacher was not easy, doing so caused the parent's confidence to grow and the relationship with the teacher to become stronger. Perhaps most important, the situation motivated the teacher to develop other approaches to discipline.

The "when I was in school" response can dictate the way you communicate with school staff. It can also propel you in a direction that may not be helpful to your child. When you make decisions based solely on your own experiences, you leave little room to view things from a broader perspective. You may also be more likely to make decisions based on the way things used to be rather than on the way things are. While experience has value, combining it with what schools currently suggest allows you to transfer the focus from yourself to your child. Hopefully, a practical approach will enable your child to benefit and you to grow. For instance, in the following situation is another parent who decided to intervene when she feared her child was being treated inappropriately, despite an inclination from her past telling her not to do so.

Joanna's mother was surprised when she heard the teacher had kept her daughter from going out to recess for several days as a means of discipline. Having a need to look into this, she and Joanna went to the teacher together. Remembering that the teacher might have had a valid reason for doing this, Joanna's mother was careful to voice her concern without attacking the teacher.

Although the teacher knew her behavior was being questioned, Joanna's mother was effective at inspiring the teacher to rethink her decision, explaining that Joanna needed opportunities to play with other children, talking over what had happened with Joanna, and resolving the issue to everyone's satisfaction.

Making a decision to question the teacher isn't easy. It was particularly difficult for this parent because she had previously had little contact with the school. But this time was different. As a child, she recalled watching other children being prevented from going out to recess. As a parent, whose child was affected, she felt driven to look into things. She wondered how her mother would have reacted. In "those days," families generally supported the teacher no matter what. A generation ago this situation might have been a nonissue; in fact, Joanna probably never would have told her mother about this in the first place.

Teachers today generally encourage families to share concerns with them. We certainly recommend that when a parent feels that a child has been treated unjustly, it is important to ask questions and investigate the issue with the teacher. (See Chapter 5 for guidelines on sharing concerns with teachers.)

What Do Families Worry About?

Regardless of time constraints, background, family structure, or values, there is a "sameness" about what families generally want for their children: to get a good education and have a good life. Going to school, a route to achieving these two goals, bears its own set of concerns. How families deal with these concerns are highly individual. The way you communicate with teachers is a reflection of how you approach these challenges.

What follows are some of the "worries" most parents experience at least once. Although many of these issues will be discussed in greater detail throughout the book, and more extensive suggestions will be offered in the remainder of the book, the approaches described in this chapter should remind you of tools you may not have considered using and help you discover confidence you didn't realize you had!

"Will my child be successful?"   Almost all parents want their children to grow up to be healthy, happy, and able to make their way in the world. As soon as you observe a sign of success (your child's ability to deal with an annoying problem or master a difficult concept), you probably breathe a sigh of relief. When you ask your child, "How did you do on the social studies test?" or "Are you getting along better with the child who sits next to you?" you hope that the response will be positive. Meeting the expectations of the school, having positive self-esteem, or showing improvement are indications of children's success. Your past experiences as well as the guidance you receive from your child's school impact the degree to which you support your child's achievements.

"How does the system work?"   This can be perplexing. Just how should you confront a problem? What staff member will be the most helpful? You may have heard stories about your friends having power struggles with the school or feeling like the "system" was not meeting a child's needs. How much do you have to become involved in order to get the best for your child? Will the school help or will you walk away frustrated? Consider the following scenario in which the teacher's judgment was questioned.

> A teacher called a parent about her daughter, saying, "I'd like to speak with you about referring Frances to the school psychologist. I've had continuing concerns about her behavior." Feeling confused because she thought Frances was doing well, the parent disagreed and questioned the appropriateness of the teacher's suggestion. Was there anyone else she should consult—another teacher or the principal? The parent didn't feel comfortable

with the situation and, after further discussion with the teacher, an arrangement was made to seek advice from additional staff.

"Why do I feel as if I'm standing alone?" "Do other parents feel the same way? Why does it always seem as though I'm the only one who is willing to speak up?" This situation arose in the following incident.

> One school principal was thinking about including multi-age classes in the school, with a combined kindergarten and first-grade classroom and a combined second- and third-grade classroom planned. The principal, who was highly supportive of the idea, asked for comments at an information session for families. One parent had reservations about the concept and spoke up, assuming others would have similar concerns. Surprisingly, no one did.

If you are frequently alone, consider the following:

- Look at the issue carefully to make sure you have an accurate understanding of it.
- You may have more time, confidence, or ability to get involved than others.
- This issue may be more important to you than others, who may share your concern but aren't prepared to become actively involved and prefer to have others take over. Or they may simply not share your sentiments.

If you have given the issue careful consideration and believe in what you are doing, then by all means stand alone.

"Will they listen to me? I, too, have a background that can be helpful."

> John Smith sat impatiently at a parent-teacher conference while the teacher described his son's unwillingness to give his best effort to his work. Smith, a professor of education

at a local college, disagreed with the teacher's recommendations to help his child and thought he knew just how his son should be handled. Should he tell the teacher what to do?

When you're in a position of having some instructional experience yourself, it's hard to know how to best advocate for your child. You may want to offer your "professional" opinion but fear giving unwelcome advice, particularly since the teacher is the one who observes the child in class and might see things differently. Consider the following:

- If you can connect on common ground, it will be easier to zero in on what is best for your child.
- Having a know-it-all attitude can intimidate teachers and put them on the defensive.
- Taking too low a profile can result in a real problem being left unaddressed.

One principal believes that anything a parent says has merit. She says, "No matter what your job, you are an advocate for your child. Saying to a teacher, 'That is not the right thing [to do]' is still advocacy."

"Am I doing the right thing?"   Regardless of the recommendations made by professionals, you may wonder, "Is this right for my child?" When you have additional support, the decision can be easier. The following illustrates one parent's dilemma.

A father was faced with a significant decision. His daughter, who had always been characterized by teachers as "socially immature" and was chronologically younger than most of her classmates, was being considered for possible retention.

After looking into all sides of the issue with school staff, it was acknowledged that the decision was a difficult one. Nevertheless, the recommendation from school personnel was to have the child repeat the year. The father thought, "What is decided now will affect her for the rest of her life. What assurance can I have that holding her back won't have negative consequences down the road?" He even thought, "Other parents not facing this don't appreciate how easy they have it. "

Realizing that the ultimate decision was his and still feeling burdened, the father reached out to others whose perspective might be helpful, including his daughter's former teacher and a friend who had also been faced with a similar decision. After much deliberation—including finding out how his daughter felt—the father agreed that his child should be retained.

Such decisions are never easy and often cause families much anxiety. But once a decision of this type is made, those involved are usually able to regroup and refocus. This results in the setting of new goals and working toward achieving them.

"How will I know if my child is slipping through the cracks?" There may be no apparent problem, yet a child may be insufficiently "stretched" to achieve. As teachers attend to the needs of the most demanding and challenging students, it is easy for them to overlook a child who meets a given level of expectations and coasts quietly along. The child who slips through the cracks may have academic, social, or emotional needs that go undetected. Those who know the child best, both teacher and family, must be sensitive to that child's needs.

Sometimes such children give signals that might indicate that they need attention, yet no one follows up on them. How many times have you heard "I hate the spelling workbook," "The teacher never calls on me," "The work is too easy," or "I never have anyone to play with at recess." When your child brings up issues like these repeatedly, you can either view them as minor but chronic concerns, or as calls for action. If you treat them as chronic concerns, you may overlook them. For some children, if these concerns are not confronted, the child may begin to drift away or fall behind. If, on the other hand, you treat them as calls for action, you will feel compelled to react and confront the issue.

As long as children are not disruptive in school, you as a parent may feel little need to ask exploratory questions. If your child says, "I hate the spelling workbook," do you reply, "That may be, but you still must use it"? This lets the situation continue and you never find out if more substantive problems are being obscured.

This is not to say that you must act on everything your child says. Some complaints do not warrant any further attention. Just saying to your child, "I'm sorry you feel this way. What makes you hate it?" is often sufficient. You are in the best position to know when your child's concerns should be pursued.

"How involved should I be with homework, especially when I don't even understand it myself?" Is it possible to help with sixth-grade math homework if you stopped understanding your child's math work when she was in fourth grade? You may wonder whether you're letting your child down if it is discovered that you can't do the work yourself.

Teachers know that families get stressed out over homework. Most teachers offer advice and guidelines as to what to do if the work seems too hard, long, or confusing for the child. The family should be viewed as a resource to the child. While acting supportive, it's best not to take responsibility for the work unless it was intended for the family to do together. (See Chapter 5 for guidelines concerning homework.)

"What are we going to hear at the parent-teacher conference?" Have you ever found yourself taking a deep breath before beginning a parent-teacher conference? You think you know what to expect, but there is always the possibility of unanticipated news. While you might dread hearing that there is something "wrong," you may also be pleasantly surprised, as in the following example.

> Vincent liked doing homework. His family always thought of him as an adequate student but never paid much attention to his school life beyond that.
>
> At a parent-teacher conference, the teacher showed Vincent's parents several recent examples of his work, all of which were impressive. Evidence of his work, together

with the teacher's comment that "His analytical thinking is far beyond the expectations for third grade," caused the parents to conclude, "Maybe he's a lot more than an OK student." The teacher continued, "With your permission, I'd like to recommend that he participate in our new enrichment activities here at school." Grinning from ear to ear, the parents responded, "Wow! We never expected a teacher to say this about our son. You can bet we will be happy to talk to him about it!"

Being pleased for Vincent, these parents left school thinking, "We must be doing something right!" (See Chapter 4 for guidelines on participating in conferences.)

"What will the teacher think of me?" While some families become involved at school, others remain at a distance. They may have concerns about the teacher's impression of their child or of themselves. The following parent had four children. She found that her interaction with school differed with each child.

> When my first child came to me with a concern, I'd say, "I'll take care of it," but I never did. With the second, my child would plead, "Don't dare tell the teacher," so I didn't. With the third, I'd become more confident, and when the teacher saw me coming, she'd think, "Oh, here she is again." By the time the fourth came along, I was ready to move into the school!

This parent's way of handling her role changed with each subsequent child. She worried less about how she was viewed, became increasingly confident in communicating with the school, and didn't hesitate to get involved on behalf of her children.

"Will the school be able to meet my child's needs?" It's hard to know whether the school is addressing all your child's needs adequately. When your child complains of too much homework or of disliking the teacher, how do you know whether confronting these issues will really solve the problem or just treat the symptoms? Should you tell your child, "Do your best with the homework," or must you look deeper? Is the teacher overburdening the class and, if so, should the teacher be made aware of it?

Surface issues can sometimes hide deeper underlying issues. As you build a trusting, working relationship with the teacher, it will be a lot easier to say, "Meg gets upset when other children are disciplined" than if you have never spoken before. In a conversation begun like this, you are more likely to discover any underlying problem than by ending the dialogue and saying to your child, "I'm sorry you hate the teacher. That's the way it is." Using a softer approach like "I'm sorry, let's see what happens today," or "If this persists, we'll have to meet with the teacher," makes it more likely that a broader issue will be revealed.

"How will I know when it is best to give up?"   Some families, when they believe in something, will persist until a situation has been resolved to their satisfaction. Others evaluate the situation, decide what is realistic for them, and at a given point will stop their effort even if they are still dissatisfied. It helps to set a target or goal with a timetable for achieving it. If you are not getting anywhere, rethink what it is you want to achieve.

Bear in mind that as much as you may believe in something, whether it focuses on the classroom or the school, you are part of a system whose goals are similar to yours even if the process through which they are achieved may differ from what you envision. It is unlikely that you will effect significant systemic change on your own. Yet, if you gather support, use a "we" approach, and have time and energy, you may be surprisingly effective. (See Chapter 5 for more information on addressing problems.)

"How much should I push for my child?"   One parent preferred to remain on the sidelines. He was supportive at home by listening to his children and letting them know that he cared. But he tried to avoid pushing. He said, "As long as I think there is nothing harmful occurring I will give my child the space to work things out independently. That is my bottom line."

Each family must do what feels comfortable. It is hard to stay in the background if you think your child is floundering. One of the most important things you can do is instill in your child the confidence and skills to speak up themselves, if appropriate, knowing that you are there for support and guidance when needed.

"What's my reputation at school?" If you habitually speak disparagingly about teachers behind their backs or are viewed as flying off the handle without checking out both sides of a story first, you risk losing your reputation as a helpful parent. After developing a pattern of consistently handling situations poorly, staff will continue to reach out to your children but may be reluctant to reach out to you.

On the other hand, if the teacher perceives that you follow through, confront your concerns openly, and base your relationship on mutual respect and honesty even when you disagree, you will still be seen as a member of the team.

Teachers don't expect parents to be human relations experts or psychologists. They understand that contacting the school is difficult for many families. But if you view every issue as an emergency or believe "I'll do anything for my child and I don't care what they think," you may get your way, but over time your reputation may be less positive than you would like.

The concerns and needs of families are vast. Parents, teachers, and other school staff are involved in working to meet children's needs in different but sometimes overlapping ways. Varying viewpoints can lead to friction and misunderstandings; even with the best intentions, conflicts can still occur. You will reduce the likelihood of these conflicts if you

- Gather all the facts.
- Listen to various sides of an issue before taking a position.
- Keep the issue between you and the teacher rather than allowing your child to get caught unnecessarily in the middle of a conflict.
- Offer positive suggestions to teachers without telling them how to do their job.
- Think of your relationship with the teacher as one of working *together* to benefit your child.

Listen Before You Speak

Schools recognize that they must be sensitive to the needs of students and their families. A successful partnership between home and school will work best if you understand that to be a good communicator you must be successful at both speaking and listening. The following thoughts, from the Wheelock College Home-School Partnership, may be helpful. [1]

> Listening is a fundamental communication skill. It is the ability to understand what someone else is saying, feeling, and/or thinking. Active listening is the ability to make the speaker feel that he/she has been heard. Communication fails if people do not feel that they have been heard.
>
> Good listening is more than a collection of skills; it stems from a particular attitude. That attitude is a real desire to understand how the other person is making sense of a situation (or how they are thinking, feeling, and interpreting). Interestingly, listening does not necessarily indicate agreement. It indicates respect.
>
> What makes listening hard is that sometimes we don't really care how the other person feels. This usually happens when we ourselves don't feel listened to or when we have too much to say. The key to listening well is being able to suspend temporarily our own need to be heard.

Here are some listening tips adapted from this work that you may wish to consider when you communicate with teachers:

> Encourage the speaker to say more. "You seem to think that my daughter isn't giving her best effort. Can you give me some examples of what you mean?"
>
> Accept the feelings of the person talking. "It must be frustrating to you to work so hard and have him not understand."
>
> Clarify and/or paraphrase what you hear. "You seem to be saying that we should be supportive at home but that we shouldn't do the work for him."

Keep your body language in harmony with your words. (Be aware of your facial expressions, the way you sit, and other aspects of your body language.)

Keep listening until there is a sign that the speaker is ready to listen to you. "What do you think?"

We suggest that you avoid:

Passing judgment on what you hear. "You're the teacher. You're supposed to be able to handle it if children don't understand."

Responding too early with your own thoughts or ideas. "I know you want to tell me more about what he's doing in class, but I think all these problems are because he needs to be in a different group."

Responding with solutions. "The answer is simple. I'm sure you will agree that her behavior will change when you let her sit with her friends."

Giving negative nonverbal cues. Don't make faces or act alarmed.

Conclusion

Effective communication doesn't come naturally to many people but, fortunately, good techniques can be learned. Communication is an important life skill, whether you are questioning a bill you have already paid or have concerns about your child getting enough time to complete an assignment. Your communication with teachers will be most effective if you believe in working with school staff toward mutual goals with mutual respect.

Notes
1. Braun and Swap, *Building Home-School Partnerships with America's Changing Families,* Boston: Wheelock College, 1987.

Chapter 2

What Makes Teachers Tick

And You Thought Teachers Had It Easy!

Think about how your day starts: milk spills, last-minute child care arrangements, and other curve balls set the tone for your day before you leave the house for work.

> Sally Jones, a fourth-grade teacher, had just left home with three of her own children—the oldest to the magnet school, the third grader to the neighborhood school, and the second grader to a private school. As they approached the car the youngest called out, "Hey, mom, the window is broken." They then found the radio was missing. Already running late, she arrived at her own school twenty minutes behind schedule and needed to use the office phone to call her insurance company. When she finally got to her classroom the teacher next door was in Ms. Jones's room trying to take attendance.

Your day, like that of Sally Jones, is typical of what the start of a day can be like for anyone. On top of all this, imagine having to put on a cheerful face for a room full of fourth graders!

Teaching poses its own challenges. Learning about what a teacher's job involves will help you develop sensitivity about what occurs beneath the surface and can assist you in maintaining a healthy relationship with your child's teacher. The following behind-the-scenes look at what teachers do will give you access to the daily demands they encounter.

Digging Into the Day

For teachers, how the day starts can dictate how the rest of the day will go. If they allow car problems and otherwise hectic households to consume them or affect classroom routines, they and their students will pay a price. Instead, teachers are called upon to put aside pressures from their personal lives as soon as they enter school. If a class starts late or if the teacher is not there to provide something the children count on, the day might never get back on track.

On the other hand, there are times when it may be appropriate for teachers to share what is happening in their lives. Without burdening students, a teacher might say, "Did I ever get up on the wrong side of the bed today!" or "The last thing I needed this morning was traffic on the thruway." These comments can bring a teacher closer to a class by demonstrating that teachers are human too. Information of this nature encourages trust. Joseph's comment that "You must hate the traffic like my mom and dad," communicates support from child to teacher.

Teachers prepare to be on duty as soon as the first student enters the classroom. Rarely spotted working at their desks waiting for children to enter the room, teachers are more likely to stand at the door ready to greet each child individually. A personal comment to each child like "Good morning, Serena. What a beautiful shirt you're wearing!" begins the day on the right foot for Serena.

Overseeing housekeeping tasks also plays a role in getting the day started. Asking for signed permission slips, reminding children to turn in their completed homework, sending the attendance to the office, collecting book club orders, and resolving the perennial missing lunch box problem are part of each morning before any actual "teaching" begins. Children frequently assist with many of these tasks themselves, freeing the teacher to focus on other things.

Doing the Teaching

It is an enormous challenge to meet children's diverse needs. Teachers are expected to follow a curriculum and at the same time recognize and address children's varying social and learning styles. In addition, there are times when the involvement of families and other school staff members is helpful in setting goals and determining programs for children.

While schools follow differing practices, teachers are generally required to prepare lesson plans that reflect curricular guidelines. Serving as the blueprint for what will happen during a given class period for the entire class, groups of students, or individual students, implementation of lesson plans can tap all of a teacher's resources. The plans may contain:

- objectives: what children will be learning, such as multiplication tables
- strategies: how learning will be accomplished, as through small groups using flash cards or computers for practice
- assessments: ways of finding out what children have learned, such as a quiz

Teachers create these plans and appropriate materials to go with them knowing that the plans are subject to change, possibly at the last minute. This may be due to a class's or student's rate of progress being slower or faster than anticipated, requiring the teacher to be flexible. Changes may also be due to other situations within the school, as in the following scenario.

> Harrison Wilkinson, a seventh-grade Spanish teacher, was about to take his class to the foreign language lab to work with videos on common Spanish phrases. Just as he was getting the key for the lab, he learned that there had been a mixup in the schedule and the lab was already being used. Disappointed and knowing the class was looking forward to this activity, Mr. Wilkinson had to quickly create another plan for his students.

Constant interruptions and delays can also effect a day's plans, forcing teachers to shift gears. A special program on drug education may cause scheduling changes, fire drills may take place, or the microscopes on loan from the science department may not arrive. Given regular occurrences such as these, teachers learn to carry out their long-term goals despite short-term interruptions.

Working with Families

Families are more visible in schools than they were a generation ago. Schools welcome and encourage notes, telephone calls, and visits to school. Families more than ever are asking questions or sharing concerns that require teachers' time and challenge their expertise. These issues will be discussed further in this and later chapters.

Additional Responsibilities

Teachers do many other things beside teach and work with families. They participate in staff development workshops, belong to school councils, give children extra help after school, and sit on other educational or community committees. Many teachers remain in school late in the afternoon long after the last bell rings, often to accommodate work schedules of families. It is not unusual for teachers to return to school in the evening to attend school concerts, plays, PTO events, or open house.

Teachers' Worries and Concerns About Children

Although it may sometimes seem to you as if you are the only one who worries about your child, be assured that the overwhelming number of teachers are concerned about your child as well. While some teachers give little effort to their job beyond their contractual hours, many more continuously reflect on your child's needs and go the extra mile. Just as you might wonder about whether your co-workers are producing the best possible product, teachers are often questioning if they are doing the best for your children. Here are some issues relating directly to your children that teachers commonly think about.

"Did Angela eat a good breakfast?"   Not feeling hungry in the morning or having to catch an early bus, she is apt to skip breakfast unless a parent encourages her to eat. As the morning wears on, the hunger pains grow. This can affect her ability to concentrate.

"Did Jamie get enough sleep?" Being allowed to watch just one more TV show can have consequences. As Jamie's eyelids begin to droop during math class the next day, can the teacher expect her to be "into" the class?

"Does Buzzy have friends?" Worrying about recess in twenty minutes and whether anyone will ask him to play basketball is a real concern for an eight year old. It can get in the way of Buzzy giving his best effort to the reading comprehension questions.

"Does Carmen know how to make friends?" Making friends, keeping them, and being part of changing friendships all play an important role in a child's life and are part of the school experience. Teachers are concerned when children are left out of a playground game or ignored in a group project. Wondering about friends at any age can stand in the way of a child's day-to-day progress.

"Does Lionel understand his job as a learner?" Children know what their job at school is—to learn. How this is accomplished may mean one thing to Lionel but something else to another child. There is a difference between waiting for the teacher to tell everyone what to do and learning how to make decisions to work independently. It is the teacher's job to create a classroom atmosphere that Lionel can develop in at his own pace.

"Is Diana happy in school?" While most children come cheerfully into the classroom each day ready for activity, Diana may find school dull. Dealing with children's attitudes toward school is a challenge for teachers. They want all children, including Diana, to feel good about school.

"How does Ralph deal with success?" What does Ralph do when he receives recognition for hard work and effort? Not every child knows how to handle success. Sometimes too much success or not knowing how to view it can get in the way of his daily progress. If Ralph isn't able to put success in the right light, meeting failure could be more difficult to handle.

"Is it frustrating for Dale when he doesn't "get it" the first time?"   Does he think he will be considered dumb if he doesn't understand fractions immediately? Children need to know that it's all right not to understand something at first. Teachers can provide different ways of handling this.

"How does Yvonne deal with conflict?"   As a fourth grader, Yvonne was upset that riding her bicycle to school was against the rules. She went to the principal. "After all," she told the principal, "I thought exercise was important." The principal explained to Yvonne the safety considerations that prevented bicycle riding to school from being allowed. If, however, other children expressed the same desire, a study group could be formed to see if changes could be made in the future.

"Is Spencer being challenged?"   Is he being pushed just enough or not enough? While teachers don't want children to be insufficiently challenged, neither do they want them to be overburdened.

"Are families sharing all the information about changes at home they should?"   Household changes—including good things—that seem minor to a parent may be significant to a child. Whether the cat has run away, parents are going through a divorce, or there will be a new baby in the family, when the school is aware of a change at home proper support can be given, which makes all the difference for a child.

Other Professional Concerns

In addition to concerns directly affecting your child, teachers think about their roles as professionals in other contexts in their work setting. The following factors affect teacher's motivation and the degree to which they are content or not content with their job. In fact, some of them may affect you in your work as well.

"How effectively will I share my expectations with parents?"   Teachers clearly understand your child's academic programs but explaining them to you can be a challenge. At one back-to-school-night, second-grade teacher Dotty Reagan told parents that she was going to change her approach to teaching reading and language. In one-to-one situations she had always articulated these changes clearly. But when a few well-meaning parents asked some difficult questions she became nervous and defensive, causing the presentation to be a disaster. For some teachers, it's easier to talk to a roomful of children than a group of adults.

"Will I be able to explain difficult news to parents?" Teachers usually try to place themselves in your family's position and provide as much support as possible, especially when sharing information that is sometimes difficult to hear. Issues such as Luke possibly needing to repeat the first grade or Molly potentially requiring an assessment to determine why her behavior has become unruly present challenges even for experienced teachers.

"What if parents are not supportive?" Teachers respect differences in the dynamics of each household. But when second-grade teacher Gordon Fogg knows that when Frederick's father doesn't ask Frederick how his homework is going or how he is doing in school, it hurts everyone. This is a worry for Mr. Fogg, who knows that a smidgen of parental concern would probably make a major difference in the way Frederick felt about school.

"Will I have job security?" In times of budgetary constraints, teachers think about their future in the profession. Contract negotiations, reduction in staff, and tenure issues all affect the way teachers view their jobs. They wonder if their salary will reflect the cost of living, if the school department will give them a voucher to pay for a graduate course, or if they will be transferred to another school or be asked to change grade levels.

"How will I get along with fellow teachers and will they appreciate me?" Most people want to fit in and be appreciated. While teachers may appear to be isolated in their classrooms, most develop supportive relationships at work and enjoy a healthy camaraderie with fellow teachers. Although each school faculty has its own "personality," many faculties think of themselves as a family.

"In what ways will I be encouraged to grow professionally?"
In all work it is important to improve one's skills. If a teacher gets into a rut, everyone suffers, particularly your child. In schools where principals supervise conscientiously and support teachers, a teacher's opportunity for growth and professional advancement will be maximized and children will benefit.

"Who will evaluate me, how often will it occur, and what will it all mean?" Many teachers become anxious when evaluations are conducted. Although supervisory and evaluation practices vary with principals, department heads, and school districts, it is natural to wonder what the principal will see during either a scheduled or a drop-in visit to a classroom. The official nature of the evaluation process can tend to give even the most secure teachers the jitters.

"Will I be provided with what I need to do my job well?"
Everyone expects to make do from time to time. In some schools, overcrowded classes, insufficient resources, and inadequate space are real problems that teachers are forced to live with. The promise of improvements may or may not come to fruition. For many teachers, creative ways of handling these deficiencies have become the rule rather than the exception.

All of the above concerns have to do with teacher's *needs*. To the extent that teachers can separate these issues from the classroom, they should not get in the way of your child's learning. But there are times when these issues can disrupt learning.

> The teachers in Kidville recently were involved in a contract dispute that resulted in a job action and teachers were advised to work only to the "letter" of their contracts but to do nothing additional.
> Michael Abrams, a third-grade teacher, had always held a "homework club" three days a week after school, and many of his students loved to go. But due to the job action he felt obligated to discontinue the club because it would require him to stay after school. This had an adverse affect on families whose children counted on the

support and the resources of the teacher. The children had to make major adjustments.

When educational opportunities are decreased, families are forced to either allow their child to go without or to be creative in seeing to it that the child is provided with the services in another manner.

Don't I Know My Child Best?

Teachers handle frustrations, conflicts, and challenges differently depending upon their experience, the community in which they teach, their own personal values, and what they learn from parents and colleagues. For example,

> At a teacher workshop, Lee Baker, a second-grade teacher, learned that spelling workbooks were just one approach to helping children learn to spell. She decided to put the workbooks aside and encourage her students to look at the way they used spelling in their everyday writing. This meant that the students would choose which words they wanted to learn.
>
> Susie's mother was very concerned about this change in the spelling program. She met with the teacher and stated, "My daughter dislikes the new approach to spelling, and I seriously question its value. I know she'll do better if you allow her to continue using the workbooks."

Here the parent is advocating one educational approach and the teacher another. Feeling secure that she knew her child best, Susie's mother was confident in asserting herself, yet may not have realized that other effective approaches to learning spelling existed.

Families are encouraged to speak up because their insights and opinions can be useful to the teacher in helping to meet children's needs. When a parent says to a teacher, "It looks this way to me. What do you think?" or "Can we talk about whether this really is the best approach for Susie?" most teachers will listen and be willing to work together. But if the parent uses the approach "This is the way I see it and this is what I want you to change," as

Susie's mother did, a successful resolution is less likely. This suggests that the parent is "telling" the teacher how to teach.

Teachers also must balance parent comments with what they think about how their child learns best with what is observed in the classroom. This can result in a teacher's perception of your child being different from your own. When differences of opinion arise, you and the teacher will be more likely to communicate effectively if you both

- Listen to each other. What information can you and the teacher share?
- Discuss goals for the child. Can you and the teacher agree on what the child needs to learn or do differently?
- Collaborate on an action plan. Determine what can be done at school and at home to support the goals established for your child?
- Arrange to check back to reassess the situation. Decide when everyone will review whether the goals are being met.
- Consider calling in a third party if issues can't be resolved between you. Request an additional school resource to become involved and provide additional insights and suggestions.

Confidentiality: When Children Share Personal Information

As you may have experienced from observing children while they play together in your home or as you carpool, many children love to chat. If you are present while they are speaking, you might inadvertently overhear children sharing personal information.

Teachers are in a similar position at school. They may be more aware of you and your family than you realize. One teacher remarked, "As children walk into the classroom they can be heard sharing all kinds of information. Often they speak in hushed voices to a friend or the teacher and are likely to comment on anything."

Here are some of the things children may say:

"My dad got a new job."

"I couldn't sleep much last night because my parents were shouting at each other. I wonder if they're going to get divorced."

"My oldest brother just got into college."

"We're moving but nobody is supposed to know."

As children get to know and trust their teachers, the likelihood that they will speak about what they hear and see from home increases. While some children are comfortable making many details about their lives public, others are not.

A classroom activity that encourages children to share such as "Show and Tell" can result in inappropriate information being divulged to the class and teacher. One child brought a plant to school (later discovered to be a marijuana plant) and enthusiastically explained how his father had many more at home! Although most teachers are careful about the questions they ask, teachers learn about personal information regularly. This places teachers in the position of being holders of sensitive data, which may cause uncertainty about how to respond. In the following scenario, the entire class became holders of information.

While having dinner, Mr. Clarkson asked his daughter Lisa, a third grader, about her day. She revealed that during a class discussion she shared everything she knew about her mother's recent surgery. Mr. Clarkson cringed as he listened and thought about how he had gone out of his way to ensure that the whole community did not hear about the surgery. Now that Lisa had told the class the details, he could imagine an onslaught of phone calls and inquiries of what-can-I-dos from well-meaning friends. This was just the kind of thing the family wanted to avoid!

Mr. Clarkson subsequently had several conflicting thoughts:

- Lisa should have known what was private and what was not.

- We should never have told her the details because children can't always decide what they should talk about in school and what they shouldn't.
- The teacher should have stopped her.
- It was our fault. Lisa had a need to talk and the classroom provided just the setting for her to vent her feelings.

Teachers try to be sensitive to family matters. There are times, as in Lisa's case, when the teacher decided it would be more harmful than helpful to stop the conversation because of the importance of the child's need to share. Yet every situation is different. One teacher said, "Certain words children use alert me to the possibility that the news about to be shared should not be made public. I can then interrupt with, 'Is this something your family wants you to share?' But teachers can't know everything. When families inform the teacher about matters at home they can more easily carry out the family's wishes."

Even when you exercise your best judgment within the family, you can't always predict what your child will share. The following situation took the teacher by surprise.

During writing period Brad and the teacher were having a conference about Brad's story. He was writing about the time his uncle came to their house for dinner as he did every Sunday. But this week was different. He was intoxicated. His loud, angry talk upset Brad's mother so much that she called the police. This scared him and his sisters.

This teacher found himself in an uncomfortable position. While needing to support Brad as he worked through his feelings, the teacher was in possession of information that appeared to constitute a private family matter.

Teachers can also get tugged in two directions when a child says, "I want to tell you what just happened to me but don't tell anyone." One teacher stated, "We have to be alert to the possibility of children sharing information that suggests abuse or neglect, which we have a responsibility to report." Confronting the fine line between respecting a confidence and the obligation to report sensitive information is part of the complexity of a teacher's job.

Teachers Receive Letters

Dear Ms. Harner,

As you know, our daughter, Stephanie, recently took standardized tests. We would like to discuss her scores. Because Stephanie has excelled in school since she started preschool and all her teachers have told us what great talent she has, particularly in math, we are anxious to know if she would qualify to participate in the enrichment curriculum for the remainder of the year.

Thank you for looking into this. We look forward to hearing from you.

Sincerely,
Joanne and David Esposito

Letters such as this ask for something. Teachers and principals receive them all the time. These letters often request that the school see things from the parent's point of view or attend to a matter that is important to them. Writing a letter to a teacher is an opportunity for you to communicate a need to the school. Consider the following in helping you draft an effective letter.

What do you want this letter to accomplish? Are you making a request, expressing a concern, or offering a suggestion?

Is it better to write a letter or make an appointment to see the teacher? This depends on the nature of the issue, your style, and what method is most practical for you. (Even if you decide to meet with the teacher, drafting a letter without sending it can also be a useful way to focus your ideas.)

In writing the letter, state your purpose right at the beginning. "I am writing this to let you know how concerned I am about the rough games that are played during recess."

Have you backed up your ideas? This is always good practice and allows the teacher to see your point of view more clearly. An excerpt from one parent's letter stated, "Mary would do better in a more advanced computer group since she uses her home computer often."

Have you reread the letter after letting a day or two pass? Review it to see if changes should be made or if you still feel strongly. It may be that your enthusiasm has diminished and your need to write the letter is not as great as you originally thought.

Think twice about the tone you establish. Phrases such as "As you know, we have done a lot for the school over the year" or "I never ask for anything but I now believe that you need to grant my request," suggest a demand and could result in making the letter less effective.

Expect a timely response. The teacher or other appropriate person should respond to you within a reasonable amount of time (generally within a week, but often much sooner). Even if they can't give you a definitive answer, or if they need to further explore an issue with you, they generally will inform you of this. If you receive no response, follow up with a telephone call.

Schools often encourage parents to write letters. One principal asked parents to write letters to school if they wished to request a particular classroom setting for their children the next year. Suggestions were made to parents as to just how to write the letter so it would focus on their child's needs.

You have the right to request anything that you feel would be beneficial to your child's well-being. Usually, letters that are brief and focused achieve the most satisfactory results.

What Goes On in the Teachers' Room?

Another aspect of the teachers' day is an opportunity for a brief time out with colleagues in the teachers' room. To nonstaff members, the closed door with the "Teachers' Room" sign has always had a mystique. Chances are that if you have walked by a teachers' room and noticed the door even slightly ajar, you have probably taken a peek inside.

Teachers' rooms usually resemble a secondhand furniture store containing a table and chairs and odd pieces of additional seating. They may also be equipped with a coffee pot, a refrigerator, or a microwave oven. Although schools vary, the room is usually used by staff for eating lunch, planning lessons, conducting small meetings, and taking brief breaks. Discussion might run the gamut from talking about current movies to debating educational issues. The following exchange is a good example of what might take place in a teachers' room:

> When Ms. White entered the teachers' room to find two trusted colleagues, she saw an opportunity to vent her hurt and anger as well as ask for advice. Mr. Bennett, a parent, had questioned her competence as a sixth-grade teacher. Mr. Bennett had almost brought her to tears.
>
> "I know how that feels," said Ms. Herrera, as she realized how upset her colleague was. "I had a similar experience with Mr. Bennett when Jason was in my class."
>
> Ms. White said, "I was only trying to discuss his son's need for extra math help after school. He made me feel as if it was my fault that Jason was having a hard time in math."
>
> Ms. White's colleagues assured her that this parent did not trust the school, and had reacted similarly with Jason's previous teachers. In addition, they suggested some ways Ms. White could help Mr. Bennett to better understand Jason's learning needs. They also advised her to tell the principal about the situation.

Although the subject of the dialogue varies, the teachers' room often serves as a safe refuge where teachers can express concerns when appropriate. This often leads to a helpful sharing of opinions and perspectives among staff. After a dose of adult talk in the teachers' room, a teacher can return to students ready to go on with the day.

When Needs and Expectations Conflict

Obviously, not all concerns are confined to the teachers' room or resolved there. Over time, teachers find that in their relationships with families, certain behaviors or attitudes can interfere with meeting children's needs. For instance, families who don't follow up with their child at home when they indicate they will, parents who give up on their children, or parents who make excuses for their children's failure to meet school obligations.

On the other hand, families also notice behaviors in teachers that they find difficult. Conflict and frustration can occur when parents feel that the teacher has homework expectations that are unreasonable, labels children negatively, or listens to a parent's concerns but does nothing about them.

Schools encourage families to be involved and communicate their concerns. Saying to a teacher that "my son James was upset because he felt you didn't think he could memorize all those lines" opens a dialogue with the teacher about the issues of confidence and prejudging children. Although what you choose to address is highly individual, by expressing concerns in a constructive way rather than suppressing them, differences can be confronted. If differences are unable to be resolved it may be necessary to seek the advice of the principal. (See Chapter 5 for guidelines in addressing concerns with teachers and Chapter 6 for guidelines in involving the principal.)

Consider the following:

- Accept that teachers will make mistakes. Whether or not you choose to confront a mistake, there is a time to forgive and look beyond it even though you may be irritated.
- Believe in teachers' potential willingness to change their actions but not their personality.
- Approach teachers with any concern, including changes at home, with the attitude that you want to work together as a team to help your child.

Conclusion

This behind-the-scenes look at what makes teachers tick assumes that teacher's needs are just as real as the needs of families. And when the needs of either are not recognized, particularly over a long period of time, frustrations are apt to develop, dissatisfaction grows, and the communication process may break down. When needs are met, the likelihood of teachers and families being in sync with each other is increased. This establishes an atmosphere where parents and teachers can communicate effectively, which ultimately benefits your child.

Chapter 3

How the School Is
Working for You

Getting Through the Maze

Most mornings, Matthew didn't want to go to his third-grade class. But once he arrived, he seemed to be fine. His work was good and his teacher was pleased with his progress.

Things at home were difficult. Matthew's father had recently moved out of the house and left Matthew with his mother and younger sisters. When the school day was over, rather than stay for any after-school activities or play with friends, Matthew came directly home and either watched television or helped take care of his sisters. Matthew's mother was concerned that Matthew's feelings about school were caused by changes in the household and all the unhappiness that led up to it.

She wondered whether she should get in touch with the school. Part of her hesitated to do anything. Worries about getting caught in the bureaucracy of the school system made her feel tugged in two directions.

Should she contact the school? Perhaps you have shared her concerns as well. After all, the huge bureaucracy that seems to exist in the school system can seem scary when observed from a distance. As you get closer, the big blur generally becomes clearer, more easily understandable, increasingly personal, and less imposing.

Rather than exist in their own worlds, staff members ideally try to work as a team to support each other and solve problems together. An important goal is to promote a sense of community among themselves as well as their students' families and their students. One experienced teacher entered the teacher's room after having a difficult morning and asked a colleague, "Will you help me figure out what I am doing wrong with my class this year?" Teachers need to reach out, collaborate, and grow.

Nevertheless, schools and the way they function can seem like mazes. And just as in a maze, experiences with your child's school may have caused you to feel as if you have reached a dead end. To avoid frustration, it helps to have an idea of the way the system works. This chapter is intended to help you understand the formal and informal ways in which many schools function.

Who's Who in Your Child's School

All schools are organized differently. Programs, policies, and staff member's tasks—including what will be taught, who will teach it, and how it will be taught—vary among schools and communities and are continuously changing. Despite these differences, schools also share certain similarities. For this reason the following overview of the roles of various school staff members, while not exhaustive, may be of assistance to you.

Professional Staff

The principal sets the tone for the atmosphere of the school. In addition to working with other administrators in the school department, most of the principal's time is spent in your child's school. Principals oversee the implementation of curriculum in collaboration with curriculum coordinators, work to expand teaching strategies, place children in appropriate classrooms, recommend the appointment or dismissal of staff, supervise and evaluate teachers, and plan how space is used. In addition, they are asked to work out the school's budget, communicate with parents, and maintain supportive relationships with the entire school community. Principals need to know how to do things, understand why they should be done, and be able to motivate staff to reach goals.

The assistant principal works with the principal in handling many of the principal's tasks and, in some cases, still retains the role of disciplinarian that you may remember. The assistant principal may also be a classroom teacher and is usually in charge of the school when the principal is unavailable.

Classroom teachers are the main link to your child's learning. In addition to "teaching," the tasks of a teacher typically require interaction with many other staff members. Asking the principal for advice, requesting that the nurse talk to the class about hygiene, or supporting an unhappy child are all part of a teacher's day. Teachers also confer with families regularly to share expectations and goals and are usually required to participate in regular workshops and staff development programs for their professional growth.

Physical education teachers, librarians, and art and music teachers often serve an entire school population. You may remember these teachers as "specialists." They, too, feel a strong sense of community with the school. Since they work with large numbers of children, it is a challenge to personalize their learning and develop trusting relationships to get to know the "whole" child within the time constraints allowed. Although these teachers work under the guidance of principals, they are often supervised by citywide coordinators in their area of expertise.

> Physical education teachers teach fundamental motor skills as well as help children understand fitness and how the body works. Children's programs may delve into areas such as health, gymnastics, sports skills, and cooperative activities. Physical education is an integral part of a child's overall development.

> Librarians work with students, teachers, and families. They may also be trained as media specialists and/or classroom teachers. At times serving several school communities, librarians help students learn to use a library and advise families by suggesting appropriate books or computer software. Librarians assist teachers by gathering books for curriculum

units or making purchases based on their needs. They also may coordinate and supervise library volunteers.

Art teachers help children transform ideas, images, and feelings into visual forms through a medium such as crayon, clay, or paint. They also help children appreciate art in various cultures as well as teach fundamentals of color, shape, and sense of order by visiting art museums, reading books, and having discussions and demonstrations.

Music teachers provide learning experiences in music appreciation through singing, creative movement, listening, music reading fundamentals, and vocal training (including breathing techniques and correct diction). Music teachers often lead a school chorus or teach instrumental lessons in addition to their other responsibilities.

English as a second language (ESL) teachers provide English instruction to children with limited English proficiency who have a first language other than English. Bilingual teachers teach subject matter to children in their first language (such as Spanish) while also developing their English language skills. Both ESL and bilingual teachers help with the cultural adjustment of students and their families to the community.

Title I teachers work in a federally funded entitlement program designed to help children learn. School systems throughout the country qualify for Title I federal funds based on the percentage of low-income families living within their school district. The children who are identified as needing supplementary support in meeting academic standards receive services. The services that are offered vary. For example, a staff member may help a teacher implement curriculum while focusing on a particular child, or a child may receive instruction in a computer lab. Title I is committed to a strong involvement with parents and may conduct workshops in areas such as helping with homework or learning about reading styles. The federal government supports states, districts, and schools in fulfilling the mandates of Title I regulations.

Social workers, psychologists, and guidance counselors help address your children's needs as they proceed through their school experience. While their training differs, many of their tasks overlap. Whether working with children individually, in small groups, with an entire class, or with families, these staff members use their area of expertise to resolve short-term or chronic concerns.

Social workers support both families and teachers. They often work with mental health centers and social service agencies in assisting families with a child or children that may be affected by difficult issues at home. As a liaison between the home and the school, social workers may interview families for assessment purposes, represent parents as mediators, help parents who are intimidated by the school feel more comfortable, work directly with children or groups of children, and assist at parent-teacher conferences. One social worker said, "Parents' worries are warranted. It is my job to help the school understand these concerns as well as attempt to resolve the issues."

Psychologists assess, evaluate, and treat social, behavioral, and learning problems. If a child has difficulty getting along with classmates, is performing poorly in school, is dealing with a change in the family, or seems generally unhappy, the psychologist can provide necessary support. After obtaining proper consent, a psychologist may talk to the child, confer with the family, consult with the teacher, and/or decide to conduct a formal evaluation. As one psychologist stressed, "Properly evaluating a child takes time. A comprehensive assessment involves consultation, observation, an interview, and often administration and interpretation of psychological and educational tools. Parents provide invaluable data and should work closely with professionals to best understand a child's individual needs."

School psychologists may also work with an entire class. In one classroom where it was thought that a child was being used as a scapegoat, role play and discussion led by a psychologist demonstrated to the class how hurtful scapegoating can be and modeled what they could do to stop it.

Guidance counselors provide short- and long-term counseling in personal, social, and academic issues to ease a child's adjustment to school. As one guidance counselor states, "Guidance [in our school] is available to every child. We teach positive interpersonal skills, which are the foundation of self-esteem."

Families, teachers, or children themselves may approach a guidance counselor for assistance. By teaching coping skills for real-life situations such as divorce or hospitalization, they also help children find ways to confront concerns around new babies, loss of jobs, or other changes in the family. Guidance counselors may coordinate standardized testing, tutoring programs, or communicate with families through newsletters.

Special educators address children's special needs by working with children and consulting with teachers to integrate the special educator's services with the curriculum and/or to teach specific skills or learning strategies. Part of this task involves diagnosing problems and developing the most appropriate strategy for a given child. A child may see one special education teacher or several simultaneously, depending on individual requirements. By problem solving together, special educators work closely with families and often are the designated liaison for students with individualized educational plans. Some special educators remain in one school all day, yet others are seen carrying their "offices" with them from school to school. Note that roles vary due to rapidly changing guidelines and regulations.

Special education teachers work with children assigned to specific programs as a result of having been identified as having special needs such as developmental delays, emotional and behavioral issues, or learning disabilities. Historically, children with significant disabilities have been placed in citywide programs where a special education teacher or staff worked with them. Recently, there has been a trend to include children, regardless of the severity of their disability, in regular classrooms in their neighborhood schools and to tie the special educators services into the context of the classroom environment. As with all teachers, special education teachers are challenged to maintain sensitivity to parent's needs and collaborate with them to reach a shared vision for the child.

Speech and language pathologists assess communication skills in children who are suspected of having language disorders, plan intervention programs to address the difficulty, and serve as resources to the classroom teacher to facilitate language learning. Traditionally, this role has focused on improving children's pronunciation. However, it also includes providing students with opportunities to engage in different types of verbal interaction such as conversation, discussions, presentations, and storytelling, and as well as working with teachers to develop a language-rich environment for all children.

Physical therapists help children who are physically challenged to function as independently as possible within the school setting. Physical therapists work with physicians and other professionals to develop programs for a child at school. For example, among many ways of helping children, exercises or available resources in the classroom may be provided to help a child improve range of motion or posture.

Occupational therapists assist children with identified limitations to function independently within the school setting. This process often involves enabling children to participate in class activities and handle their own self-care needs through the use of adaptive equipment such as table easels, eating utensils, and handwriting aids. While some occupational therapists work with children out of the classroom, others focus on working with children in the classroom. One occupational therapist noted that "Occupational therapist services are becoming increasingly effective in the classroom setting by developing goals in consultation with families and other professionals."

Gifted student educators. In some school systems, the needs of high-ability students are met by placing them in settings where staff develops programs and expectations that are different from those of regular classrooms. School systems design these pro-grams, with collaboration from administrators, principals, and teachers. Entrance to such programs may require screening proce-dures such as testing or interviews. Students may become part of an entire class, sometimes across town in a different school, or may be taken out of their regular classroom for specific time peri-ods in a separate location at their school.

Another approach to meeting the needs of such students is for the classroom teacher to be encouraged to develop innovative ways to address the needs of all students, including those who may have high ability, and for curriculum to be written to contain "challenge" activities.

School nurses provide services such as hearing and vision testing, immunizations, and scoliosis screenings. In addition to using assessment skills to decide how "real" a tummyache is, nurses administer a broad spectrum of medications that have been pre-scribed by children's physicians. Nurses also take advantage of opportunities to teach, either in their office or as part of a class-room program. Even a cut finger can provide a chance for a child to learn about hygiene.

School nurses are often employed by local health depart-ments and frequently serve several schools, often with the assis-tance of trained health aides providing backup coverage when the school nurse is unavailable. For those new to the community, nurses can refer families to available resources.

Aides assist teachers or other school staff. They may work with a single child, a small group, or an entire class. Some aides may be certified teachers who choose to assist other teachers rather than have classrooms of their own. If necessary and appropriate, aides may also serve as substitute teachers. Teachers value the assistance of aides, particularly the individual attention and additional sup-port they are able to give children.

Support Staff
The following staff members also meet your children's needs. Just as schools have variation in their professional staffs, support staffs differ as well.

Secretaries are usually your first contact when entering the school office. By having a finger on the pulse of the entire school, the secretary helps you communicate with the staff and your child when necessary. As one secretary says, "It's the simple things we do that can make a difference." When a secretary calls a parent to say that her daughter received the telephone message and she knows to come straight home from school, this is comforting to the parent and it builds relationships. The ability of the school secretary to make you feel comfortable, even when things are hectic, can send an important message that promotes good feelings between the school and the community.

Custodians may maintain the heating, ventilation, and air conditioning systems and take care of lighting and cleaning the school. Beyond their already full day, custodians connect with the school community in their own personal style, often greeting children with a special "good morning." In cooperation with the principal, the custodian also plays a key role in ensuring overall school safety. With a goal of keeping everyone at school accident-free, the custodian anticipates and prevents hazards or arranges for their repair when they exist.

Food personnel may include food handlers, lunchroom attendants, or food managers, with each role having separate tasks. Generally, food handlers work with food at a central location and then distribute it to the schools. The food is either prepared from scratch or provided by a food company. After children receive their food, they may be supervised by lunch or breakfast attendants during their eating period. Attendants work under the supervision of a manager, one of whose roles is to assist families whose children require special diets. Food managers often take care of bookkeeping and ensure that the food preparation is carried out in accordance with federal requirements. Having to service many children, frequently within a short period of time, is a challenge to all food personnel.

Additional Staff
Substitute teachers take over when the regular classroom teacher is absent. The substitute is expected to follow the teacher's plans for the day or use a "substitute folder" containing scheduling

43

information, books to be used, and special lesson plans provided by the teacher. Substitutes may be new to the profession, waiting for a teaching position to become available, or former teachers returning to the classroom. They may also be hired as permanent "subs" who report to a given school each day and work in classrooms as needed.

Contrary to a common perception that a substitute's presence signals an unproductive day, substitutes can offer innovative approaches and provide students with valuable learning experiences. Even when substitutes are asked to teach a subject with which they are unfamiliar, they can use imaginative strategies to help children grow. By encouraging children to work together, quiz each other, work on research projects, or even do the homework together, the experience can be positive.

Student teachers are sometimes called interns. They are sent to your child's school from local colleges and universities to have hands-on experience in the classroom. Initially, student teachers may observe in the classroom. They gradually increase their involvement, eventually taking over the entire class for a given time period. In addition to learning from experienced teachers, student teachers provide opportunities for their mentor or cooperating teachers to reflect on their own teaching practices and grow themselves. As one cooperating teacher stated, "Having a student teacher puts the classroom teacher in the position of thinking through the whys of their own teaching."

Community volunteers provide invaluable assistance to the school community. Working sometimes on a daily basis in a classroom, volunteers offer special skills, time, and support. (See Chapter 7 for information on volunteering in schools.)

School Communication

Schools must have structures to ensure regular communication between and among staff members and families. Although school communities vary in these structures, some of them may include:

Central Administration

Your child's principal communicates with the superintendent, assistant superintendent, coordinators, and other staff members in the school department. These staff members are part of the "central administration." The principal also keeps in contact with other principals within the school department, usually through regularly held principals' meetings. Often led by other administrators, principals' meetings provide opportunities for dialogue in areas such as curriculum, class size, budgetary concerns, the needs of students, or ways to enlist family involvement.

Attendance at professional conferences or other meetings is also required of your principal and other staff members. It is important that opportunities exist for communication and learning beyond what occurs in your child's school. This interaction provides a link between the needs of a particular school and the goals and expectations of the entire school and educational system.

Staff Meetings

Regular staff meetings held at your child's school are usually directed by the principal but often invite staff participation. The structure of the meetings depends on the leadership style of the principal. One principal asked the faculty to divide into groups by grade level to develop what they would want to see as a homework policy. Another principal developed a policy first, presented it to staff, and then asked for the staff's thoughts.

While the frequency of the meetings and topics to be addressed varies, they might include discussion of new programs, school policies, or discipline strategies. In addition to classroom teachers, other professional staff who work in the building may be asked to attend faculty meetings.

The staff is also routinely asked to attend professional development programs or workshops, which may be organized by the district and held on "early release" or "in-service" days or at regular times throughout the school year. Typical workshops might focus on "Using Technology in the Classroom," "Meeting the Needs of All Children," or "Looking at the First-Grade Social Studies Curriculum."

Small Committees

A principal or other administrator may form a subgroup to study a particular area of concern. This subgroup may include members of the staff, parents, or other community members. One school had a need to study school safety, particularly around dismissal. The group consisted of teachers, parents, the school safety officer, and a custodian. After working together for several weeks, the group reported their findings and recommendations, which eventually became the basis of new safety regulations at the school.

Over the past few decades, decision making regarding school issues has enlisted increasing community involvement. Schools that establish their own policies and expectations with the assistance of the wider community are an energizing vehicle for deliberation. School administrators and other staff members in collaboration with community participants may reach a broad spectrum of school-related decisions by working with committees. Developing models for report cards, creating programs around respect for human differences, or defining core values illustrate a few areas upon which such committees may focus.

Day-to-day Interaction

You may not realize the frequent contact staff members have with each other concerning your child. One staff member talking to another outside a classroom door is most likely to be discussing such topics as "How did you get Amy to bring in her homework last year?" Although this contact may seem to take place in casual settings such as school corridors, the lunch room, or the parking lot, this communication can provide vital assistance in meeting your child's needs. It is not unusual, for instance, for an art teacher to use planning time to meet with a classroom teacher to discuss a child's progress.

Staff members must also communicate with each other about other forms of vital information. Upon learning of a newly diagnosed diabetic child, a school nurse should speak to the physician, the child, and the family as well as the child's teacher so that through a process of education all involved can become comfortable with the situation. As one teacher in just such an incident remarked, "Without spending time with the nurse, I would have been anxious. I now am more knowledgeable and can better support my student."

Parent Groups

The PTO (or in many areas called the Parent-Teacher Association or PTA) is the most widely known parent group in the school community. It is an organization that helps families and the school by working together to benefit your child. The PTO develops programming for the school community, organizes fund-raising events, discusses school issues, provides information to families, and organizes volunteer assistance for the school. (See Chapter 7 for further discussion of the role of the PTO.)

The school community also operates beyond the school building. School councils (advisory groups consisting of educators and families who collaborate to study issues and establish school policy aimed at school improvement), school foundations (nonprofit community organizations that raise money for the schools), and school committees work toward getting the best for your child. In some communities, town meetings have become a setting for the citizenry to learn, share, and reach decisions about school issues.

Individual Involvement

The most effective and inclusive school atmospheres are those that respect the value and important contribution of each member of the whole school community.

Unofficial Outreach

Saying Something Special to a Child

By reaching out beyond the job description, a teacher's effort can go a long way. Things happen spontaneously that families never hear of, often causing children to feel wonderful. One teacher said, "It's where we really make a difference."

> Charles was about to walk through the double doors when he saw his last year's teacher almost pass by him. Instead, she stopped short and asked, "Charles, it's so good to see you. I've missed you this year. Tell me, how are you finding math?"
>
> At first Charles thought, "Oh, no, what did I do? What does she want?" When he realized that his previous

teacher was sincerely interested in how he was doing, he felt like a giant. "She cares about me when I'm no longer in her class." A big smile came over Charles. He now knew to expect that when teachers stopped him in the corridors they didn't always have discipline on their minds. They also could make kids feel terrific!

This teacher expressed her interest in this child in more than generalities. Charles got the message that his previous teacher still cared about his progress. This boosted his self-esteem and sense of belonging at school.

Telephone Calls to Families

Although it may not formally be required of teachers, school administrators generally expect that staff will use the telephone as a method of communication between home and school. By using the telephone, families and school can become accessible to each other. But have you ever been caught by surprise and experienced a situation similar to the following?

> "Hello, Chris. This is Mr. Blane. If either your mother or father is at home, may I speak to one of them?"
>
> Chris says, "Uh, yeah, I guess so. Hold on a minute." With his hand over the phone he beckons to his father, points to the telephone, and fearfully mouths, "It's my teacher!"
>
> The father walks to the phone with some surprise. "Hello, Mr. Blane. Is something wrong?"

The father and child were concerned. This may have been due to the teacher not having called previously or calling only when there was a problem. If you receive an unexpected telephone call from any staff member, it may be helpful to note that

- The school may want to contact you for any number of reasons. Many are neither good nor bad. Often the staff member needs or wants to ask a question, share an observation, or discuss an ongoing situation. Because

48

teachers know that families worry about calls from school, many try to begin by assuaging any anxiety— "Hello, Mr. Smith. This is Joseph Jones, Malcolm's teacher. Everything is fine and Malcolm is doing well, but I'd like to ask you a question."

- Individual teachers set the tone for telephone call practices. If a teacher offers a home telephone number, use it when you think you should. It represents that teacher's way of reaching out to connect with families. Many teachers call home periodically to give updates of children's progress. If told about this ahead of time, you will become accustomed to calls from the teacher and view them as positive opportunities to share.

Spontaneous Parent Groups

When a situation becomes emotional, everyone affected can get involved. Working with the teacher, the principal, or others in deciding the best route to take, things can happen both simultaneously and spontaneously. Perhaps you have become involved in a situation like this:

Sherry's sixth-grade teacher gave lots of tests. The class accepted the idea that they were going to have many tests that year. But when the students observed a testing strategy they found to be unfair, parents got involved and the teacher was requested to rethink her methods.

Before the first few tests, the teacher would review. The teacher specifically told the class what would be asked. But when the test was passed out, additional questions were added. Thinking this was unfair, many students began to tell either the teacher how they felt verbally or write respectful notes on the tests explaining that they did not feel responsible for extra questions. Those who got them wrong had points taken off. The teacher responded to student's concerns by saying, "You should know this information anyway."

Parents of these students began making telephone calls to each other to decide how to proceed. They questioned the teacher (which proved ineffective) and, with the teacher's knowledge, also spoke with the principal.

The parents reached out among each other to determine how to get the problem solved. With the assistance of the principal, the teacher eventually realized that she was saying one thing and doing another. She was willing to stop asking questions beyond those she agreed would be on the test. (See Chapter 6 for guidelines on bringing a problem to the principal.)

It's Hard Enough to Find the Office

With many staff members continuously flowing through schools, it is easy to have an us-against-them attitude or be intimidated by those who are unknown to you. It is easy to think, "I can only rely on myself, and they all have each other." However, if the goal of the school system is to support the entire school community by working together, you are part of this community. Think of your child's school staff as most effective when they work with families as a team.

Whom Do You Contact?

Almost everyone wants to be helpful to their child, but they also want to accomplish things quickly. Interestingly, what might seem to be the shortest route can become the longest, and what appears to be the longest can become the most effective and efficient.

Going to the classroom teacher first is sound advice. While it may not be possible for the classroom teacher to provide all the assistance you require, it is still in your child's best interest for the teacher to be aware of your concerns and be given an opportunity to address them.

Yet there will be times when first going to someone other than the classroom teacher can also be appropriate. You might do this if a concern originates in places such as the gym, the playground, at lunch, or at home. Even when you're not sure whether there is a problem, you may need advice from a staff member other than the classroom teacher.

Staff should be happy to speak with you if you are looking for general information or guidance relating to their area of expertise. However, in many schools these relationships will be encouraged to remain short term unless it is in the child's best interest for other school personnel to become involved as well. This approach to the process is consistent with the philosophy of the school operating as a team.

In making decisions about whom to contact, your style, your child's personality, the staff member involved, and the atmosphere of the school will play a role in dictating your approach. For instance, in the following case a parent decided to approach the social worker rather than the teacher:

> When Diana witnessed her father's temper lead to a physical assault on her mother, the mother was worried about the affect this would have on Diana and brought her concern directly to the school social worker. It was handled in a few sessions. In addition, outside counseling was recommended for the parents, which over a period of time, appeared to be effective. As one social worker has noted, "When parents come to me, they often need support with their own problems as much as with their children's."

It can be difficult to decide whom to contact. Should Diana's mother have gone to the psychologist, the social worker, or someone else? Although she chose the social worker, the psychologist may also have been appropriate.

Don't worry about approaching a staff member who is not able to help you. Most school staff are clear about what they're comfortable handling and what is beyond their area of expertise. They will be able to recommend who is best suited to guide you.

The following suggestions will help you decide whom you should initially contact:

State your concern to yourself in one sentence.   "I'm worried that children are getting too rough riding home on the bus," "The discipline problems in that class seem to be getting out of hand," or "My child is just coasting." By summing up the situation, you will clarify what needs to be investigated.

Determine where something happened and who was on duty. Was it in the gym, the playground, the resource room, or at home? Was the music teacher in charge or was it the classroom aide? Sometimes this information will help you decide whom to contact first.

Consult your school handbook, if one is available. Your child's school may publish a handbook similar to a yellow pages directory that lists services your school provides and the names of staff members who provide them. This resource can be of value in educating you about your options. By reading a staff member's title ahead of time, you can feel more comfortable making an initial contact. Note that staff members mentioned in this book frequently service more than one school and may not be at your school every day.

Is there someone with whom you have had contact and already feel comfortable with who might provide initial assistance or direction? One parent remembered feeling especially supported by a staff member who had guided her through a difficulty with her older child two years earlier. This parent thought, "I felt I could trust him. I liked the kinds of things he said. I think I'll give him a call to see if he can help me."

Although this person was ultimately not the one who offered long-term assistance, he served as a trusted resource at the time the parent needed a good listener and was able to redirect the parent successfully.

Make contact with the school resource who seems to fit your needs. One mother was concerned that her daughter was unfairly denied being a gym leader for her class. By going directly to the physical education teacher, it was discovered that there had been a misunderstanding and the situation was remedied.

However, questions about schoolwide matters such as the mainstreaming of all children with significant disabilities into regular classroom settings also may arise. In this instance, it may be appropriate for a parent to contact the principal or a special educator. This way the parent can ask questions and learn about varying aspects of the issue.

Despite your best effort, however, you still may be guided to someone different from the person you first contact. For instance,

> William's mother noticed that he had begun to stutter. She felt certain that by talking to the speech therapist, he quickly would be given special exercises that would improve his stuttering. The speech therapist felt that this concern first required further investigation. After consulting with the classroom teacher and the family, further inquiries led to the identification of a more involved problem. A combination of staff members, including the school psychologist, were able to meet William's needs over time.

The parent used her best judgment, but the process differed from what was originally anticipated.

Place a note in a staff member's mailbox. Staff members are not always easy to reach. State your concern in the note or simply ask to be called back. You can deliver the note to the individual's mailbox at school or call the office and ask the secretary to write the message for you. Be sure to leave your phone number indicating when you can be reached. If your phone call is not returned within a day or two, call again. The school secretary should be able to tell you what days a particular staff member will be in your building.

You can also contact staff members while they are at another school. For example, the mother of a fifth-grade flute player was unsure of her daughter's lesson time that afternoon. Unable to reach the flute teacher at her daughter's school, the mother found out what school the teacher was visiting and contacted the teacher there. This was appropriate. However, if the situation is not urgent, it's best to wait until the teacher is due to visit your school.

If Your Child Needs a Formal Assessment

Throughout your child's school career, you will have many contacts with the school. Either you or the school may identify a concern that requires your involvement in designing a plan to meet your child's needs. Consider the following note sent home to a third grader's mother.

Dear Ms. Merrill,

   As you know, we've both been concerned about Donald's behavior in class for quite some time. I've worked with him, and I know you have as well. After our conference last week, and after talking to the school psychologist, it seems that the best approach would be to consider referring him for an assessment so that we can all have a clearer direction as to how to best meet Donald's needs.

   Kindly call me at school or make an appointment to come in so that we can talk.

Best regards,
John Dillard

Letters like this are not easy to receive. Often a teacher and family have worked together to help the child or a teacher has been in contact with and sought advice from other staff members such as a child study team, yet the child's progress remains unsatisfactory. It may then be appropriate to seek a broader appraisal of a child's learning needs through a formal assessment. The process by which this occurs varies in communities. An approach similar to the following may occur in your community:

- A teacher fills out a referral form with the parent's knowledge. It requests a description of a child's progress in several areas including what has already been tried.

   How has the child progressed in subject areas (e.g., math or social studies)?

   Under what conditions does the child learn best?

   How does the child get along with peers and adults?

   How well does the child understand and remember?

   How well does the child express written and oral concepts?

   How are the child's gross-motor skills (as demonstrated in physical education) and fine-motor skills (e.g., handwriting)?

   What is the child's attitude and overall classroom behavior?

What does the child enjoy doing?

What are the areas of major concern?

- This information is shared with a team of staff members that might include the principal, psychologist, social worker, reading specialist, classroom teacher, or others. They conduct an initial assessment to see if the child requires special services.
- Information gathering takes place. The school makes recommendations for an assessment related to a child's suspected need. For example, if a child appears to have a reading difficulty, reading testing would be recommended. If a child has poor listening skills, auditory processing testing may be advised. In addition, the school or family may request additional testing such as a health, psychological, or home assessment.
- The family gives consent for any planned testing. This decision is based on recommendations that the child's team of professionals previously identified.
- An assessment is conducted and the results are explained at a team meeting, that the parents, as members of the team, are invited to. It may be determined that the child does not have "special needs" but has areas of weakness that can be addressed by the classroom teacher. However, if the child does have special needs, an individual educational plan (sometimes abbreviated as IEP) is proposed for the child. It is the family's written consent that sets the program in motion.
- At this point the program begins for the child. The process will include periodic reviews and communication with staff, family, classroom teacher, and child in an effort to determine how it is working.

The Emotional Demands on Families

Despite everyone's best intentions, once you discover that your child has a special need, you may find that this places you on an emotional roller coaster. There are decisions to be made about programs, evaluations, and general involvement in a complex system. You also may be uncertain about whom to contact and when and how to reach that person. This process takes time and can drain your energy, especially when you have to attend to other family needs. Perhaps the system is or appears to be blocking progress rather than encouraging it. You may have even greater concerns. It is not unusual to think

"What caused my child to have this need?"

"Why can't things be accomplished more quickly?"

"I feel as if the whole staff is ganging up on me."

"This child is not achieving as well as his siblings."

"These teachers can sit at their desks and tell me what is wrong with my child. How would they feel if it were their child?"

If you have these concerns you should share them with school personnel rather than allow them to fester. If you can say to a teacher, "I know this support is planned to help my child, but it's hard for me to accept that it is necessary," you have taken a critical step in developing a trusting relationship with that teacher. If the teacher says, "I can understand how you feel. After all, we all want our kids to get through school easily," you are likely to then believe that the teacher understands. One parent told a teacher, "I have always been advised not to trust the experts." This teacher worked hard to win her confidence. It is important that these concerns be raised. If you have unresolved issues they will detract from your effectiveness in helping your child. It is the teacher's responsibility to help you resolve these concerns.

Although some of the following suggestions apply to relationships with any teacher, most are designed to be helpful to you when dealing with special education issues.

- Question what you don't understand. If the teacher uses shop talk or educational jargon you don't know, question what it means. One teacher said, "I have to be alert to parents who say, 'Yes, Yes,' when I know they are unclear about what is being proposed for their child."

- Be patient. It often takes longer than many parents initially think to bring a child up to grade level, even when the child is just slightly behind.
- Respect the team approach. One skeptical parent said, "It's disconcerting to sit in this meeting knowing everyone is talking about your child." Although it might be easier to work with fewer people, group decisions are often the most effective.
- Be realistic about the expectations you have for your child. One parent said, "We now realize that we will be happy with small indications of growth rather than large ones." In addition, since not all problems can be remedied, you and your child may need to learn skills for coping with varying disabilities.
- Place yourself in the teacher's position, just as teachers should attempt to place themselves in yours. One special education teacher said, "Being able to see things through parent's eyes and identify with them is key to building good relationships and successes with children. It takes time to develop trust, but once you do it, the bond can be very strong." Also, try to acknowledge the teacher's effort even when success is not obvious to you.
- Stay informed about support groups, parent advisory committees, or other resources such as advocates. They can provide you with guidance in helping your child.
- Read brochures usually available through the school that explain your rights as well as the entire special education process.
- Be persistent. As one special education administrator advised, "If you are not achieving a resolution, pursue it until it is addressed. Doing this builds trust and provides for a climate of open communication and respect."

The Staff Pulls Together

Unforeseen situations can challenge school staff members to act quickly. If the unexpected occurs, the degree to which staff members jump to attention and work together can be similar to a scene in a hospital emergency room—everyone needed pitches in. Each person involved must be able to relate to and communicate with others for complex issues to get resolved successfully.

The following scenario illustrates how this can become necessary as those involved form an immediate team to confront and resolve the situation.

> Tim was a sixth grader who seemed to be well liked by everyone. Unfortunately, over a period of time he had developed behavioral and academic difficulties. Among other things, his mother had told him since he was a toddler that his father had gone away but someday would come back to see him. Tim and his mother were being seen by several members of the professional staff at school.
>
> One day, Tim seemed to snap. While sitting in his social studies class on the second floor and with no apparent provocation, Tim announced, "That's it. I've had it. I'm out of here." He bolted out the door and ran down the stairway. The teacher and the class observed him from the window, running down a busy city street, soon to be out of sight.
>
> The stunned teacher used his classroom intercom to call the office and report what had happened. Tim's behavior set off a series of responses, affecting many.

When the incident took place, the following people needed to think things through on their own as well as communicate with others. This was necessary not only in finding Tim but in working together afterward on Tim's overall situation.

The Classroom Teacher.   The teacher needed to make an immediate decision about what constituted proper procedure. Although a child may never have run out on him before, he knew this was a time to call for help. He also thought, "Did I do anything to provoke Tim to do this? We thought Tim was making progress, but I wonder if this behavior is an indication that we're all missing something."

The Principal.   As soon as the call came into the office, the principal took responsibility for seeing to Tim's return. Knowing his first priority was to ensure Tim's immediate safety, the principal acted quickly in deciding whom to contact and how to proceed.

The Students in the Class.   While their first reaction was to laugh at what had happened, they also, worried about Tim. It frightened them to observe their teacher reacting to such an event and to witness their classmate doing something they knew was wrong.

The Police.   It was apparent to the principal that the police needed to be contacted to look for Tim using their expertise and experience. Their goal was to find him and prevent him from being harmed.

Tim's Mother.   Learning that her son had run away from school was shocking. Already under stress, this situation exacerbated the mother's worries about Tim and the way Tim dealt with his anger.

The School Psychologist.   "How are we going to handle him once they find him and bring him back?" thought the psychologist. By examining his records and conferring with other staff members, the psychologist tried to make sense out of Tim's recent behavior and find an explanation for why he left the class.

The Social Worker.   Her immediate concern was to "just let him get returned safely," but her focus soon shifted to wondering whether she had met with the mother frequently enough. The social worker also questioned whether it might be necessary to consider a referral to an outside agency that could give additional support to Tim and his mother.

Fortunately, this incident had a favorable ending. Tim was found in good condition by the police and returned to school. After the principal spoke with the staff, his mother, and Tim, the boy was returned to the classroom. The cooperative effort of school staff helped resolve this crisis and brought Tim back to a status where he was making progress.

This scenario illustrates how Tim's behavior involved several school and community resources. While most children would not run away from school, it is not unusual for children to act out in varying ways during the school day, which may require the assistance of multiple staff members acting as a team.

When Communication Breaks Down

Despite good intentions, interactions with the school for any purpose don't always result in satisfaction or happy endings. While some may have had experiences in which the school staff has worked together as a closely knit team, others may have found school organizations to be overly bureaucratic and difficult to negotiate. One parent told another, "I can't believe how the school messed up over something as simple as getting the forms signed!" More likely, you may have experienced the process of working with the school as not totally ineffective or effective but a combination of both. In the best managed organizations, communications and the "system" can fall short of your expectations. This may happen for the following reasons:

With so much to do, things get missed. Important information is not always communicated.   Notices from the office pass teachers' desks all day. At the end of one busy day, the teacher didn't see the folded slip of paper with Raymond's name on it from the music department. It was a permission slip allowing him to play with the school band at the city hall on Veteran's Day that week. Last minute attempts to get permission failed and Raymond didn't perform at city hall. Although oversights like this don't happen often, children can lose out when adults make mistakes. When the teacher realized what had happened, she changed her system of giving students' messages and apologized to Raymond and his family.

It is not always easy to ask for assistance.   Sometimes it is difficult to admit to oneself that it is time to reach out for help. Have you ever noticed a tendency to want to do it all yourself? Teachers can be the same way and may even wonder if seeking help will be perceived by colleagues or superiors as a sign of inadequacy. They feel they should be able to solve every problem on their own.

One teacher believed a child's reading comprehension would improve as he matured. This didn't happen. The next year the child's teacher noted a reading problem early in the year and additional support was deemed necessary. The child's father had difficulty accepting the previous teacher "missing" his child's reading problem. He said, "If this had been nipped in the bud, Joey might be more comfortable reading in class." By not sharing information with the parent, the teacher prevented an opportunity for a joint decision to be made.

Following through is very important. When responsibilities are not clearly defined, there is always a possibility that the process will break down due to an assumption that "the other person will take care of it." Lack of an understanding of expectations or lack of commitment can result in things not being addressed. What follows is an example illustrating a teacher's lack of follow through.

Jesse complained to his teacher that he was being chased by older students on the playground before school. She was unclear who was responsible for children at that time of day, if anyone. Aside from showing empathy, she did little to investigate or come to Jesse's aid. She assumed he'd tell his family and they would look into things. The teacher remarked, "I try not to worry about the kids who are out there early. I know they're there but there's not much I can do."

The situation worsened. One morning, Jesse came into class crying. Still not believing the responsibility for handling the situation was hers, the teacher finally passed the problem on to the principal.

This harassment could have been stopped much earlier than it was. By not responding promptly, the teacher provided no help to Jesse until it was obvious that she had to act. Jesse would have suffered less if the teacher had followed through immediately.

It is not only staff who don't always follow through. Families can disappoint staff as well. The partnership works best when families, school personnel, and children each clearly understand what is expected of the other. When expectations are not clear or when assumptions are made incorrectly, things get missed and needs are not met.

Useful Hints About School Staffs

Communication with school staff can be easier and more productive if the following hints are kept in mind.

- The climate of many schools supports lots of internal communication among staff unless you are providing a staff member with confidential information. They find this openness ultimately helps students.

- Schools need you to tell them when things aren't working for you or if something doesn't seem right. They expect that if you have a concern, even a small one, you will share it with the classroom teacher or another staff member. Don't feel that something must develop into a major problem before you contact the school.

- If you bring a concern to a staff member and it has already involved others, give this person information about what steps you have taken so far. For instance, if you call the school psychologist and have already spoken to the social worker and the principal, let the psychologist know. By having all the background information, the psychologist will be in a much better position to advise you and your child.

- Many staff members have supervisors who are usually based outside your child's school, often in the central administration building of the community. While the staff members are technically responsible to the building principal, their direct supervisor is usually a professional who has particular expertise in their field. For example, the bilingual teacher will work with students at your school and will be responsible to the principal, but the teacher may be directly supervised by the director of bilingual education.

- The team approach with the principal as coach and everyone else working together sets the collegial tone that includes you and your children. Obviously, there are times when even the most collaborative school atmospheres become bureaucratic in their expectations. The idea of going through red tape is an unwelcome yet unavoidable reality that sometimes has to be lived with.

- If you are unsure about who to contact, ask your child's classroom teacher for advice.
- Schools want to hear from you when there are changes at home. Problems arise when changes occur and the child is affected in school. If information has not been shared with the school, it is more difficult for the school to support the child. Even if you are uncomfortable sharing specifics, it is helpful to simply say to the teacher, "This is a stressful time."
- There are some things that your child's school and teacher can't remedy on their own, such as redistricting decisions. Such issues are often resolved by the joint effort of the community and the central administration.

Conclusion

If you have a concern about your child's school experience, *do something*. It is appropriate to ask questions and work with the school in order to resolve it. The background information in this chapter should help you to get advice and make decisions more easily. While schools want families to communicate with them and should support you regardless of your knowledge of the system, you can more easily help yourself and your child with some basic comprehension of schools and how they work.

Chapter 4

How to Develop the Parent-Teacher Relationship and Keep Things Running Well

The Importance of Trust Between Families and Teachers

Have you ever faced a situation similar to this?

> Kate's mother, Beverly Arno, is worried that Kate has no friends in her first-grade classroom. By November she has not had an after-school play date with any classmates, although she has played with children in other classes. Ms. Arno mentions this to Ms. Farrell, Kate's teacher, during a routine conference. She is careful to express her concern without being demanding. "I'm worried about Kate feeling lonely," she says. "I'm wondering if there's anything that could help the situation."
>
> Ms. Farrell, always concerned about socialization of young children, had not particularly noticed that Kate lacked friends, but she considers Ms. Arno's comments. After observing Kate more closely she decides that Kate may, in fact, be feeling left out. She decides to take special care in placing Kate in groups with those children who seem to like and get along well with Kate. In addition, if Ms. Farrell notices that a classmate and Kate have clicked, she encourages the relationship. Ms. Farrell is able to use Ms. Arno's insights to Kate's advantage.

The key to a good relationship between parent and teacher is trust. This trust does not develop automatically. It is carefully created and nurtured through good rapport and respect. When teachers see that parents are dependable, honest, and credible, they can feel free to be honest and open and will work hard on your child's behalf.

If a parent's behavior engenders distrust, however, the teacher may be less likely to make an extra effort on the child's behalf. For instance, if a parent habitually approaches the principal, without first sharing concerns with the teacher or speaks against the teacher publicly, the parent-teacher relationship could become irrevocably damaged. Not only will the parent-teacher relationship be hurt, but the real loss may be the child's, as in the following:

> Thomas McKnight, a fourth-grade teacher, and John Clark, a physical education teacher, are in the teachers' room for a coffee break. During their casual conversation Mr. Clark says, "Hey, I heard you were kind of tough on William Paulson the other day. His mother told me at soccer practice that William said you had yelled at him in front of the class. William can be kind of high spirited, can't he?"
>
> Even though Mr. Clark doesn't mean to confront Mr. McKnight or spread gossip, Mr. McKnight is shocked. He thinks, "Why didn't William's mother ask me about this directly? Why did she have to complain to Mr. Clark? I wonder if she said anything to the principal at the PTO meeting the other day. I did speak firmly to William, but for good reason. I'm at a loss as to how to help him, and he has so much to offer."

Ideally, Mr. McKnight shouldn't let this incident influence him. However, in reality, it could make him self-conscious and hesitant in his interactions with William and prevent student and teacher from developing a friendly, easygoing relationship. William may then feel uncomfortable asking questions or requesting extra help.

The parent-teacher relationship works best when trust between parents and teachers is mutual. As you may note in the situation above, it is possible to inadvertently say or do things that interfere with achieving that trust.

Building trust can be viewed as a learned skill and it requires your effort as well as the teacher's; any attempt you make to achieve trust is worthwhile. Comments to a teacher such as "Let me know how I can help you," "Call me at work," or simply making eye contact are important because they demonstrate that you are connecting with the teacher. If you view building trust as an important process, it will become not only relatively easy but also will ultimately benefit your child's school experience.

This chapter will help you succeed in building trust, and in maintaining and maximizing your relationship with your child's teacher as the school year progresses.

Getting Off on the Right Foot

There is an excitement in the air at the beginning of a new school year. Teachers ask, "Will I ever be ready?" Parents wonder, "Is this the right teacher for my child?" Children may worry, asking "Who will my friends be?" As opening day jitters wear off and the year begins to unfold, the following suggestions will help you set a positive tone to your relationship with your child's teacher.

Try to avoid prejudging a teacher. Each teacher-student relationship is unique. Give every teacher a fair chance even if you've heard rumors from other parents. You may not know the whole story. If another parent's assessment of an experience with a teacher is negative, it doesn't mean yours will be—even if that parent is a friend or someone whose opinion you respect.

> Mr. Gill, a sixth-grade teacher, believed in homework— and lots of it. He had quickly earned a reputation as the "homework ogre." When Ted found out he would be in Mr. Gill's class, he worried about his ability to keep up. Privately, his parents did, too. But they kept their concerns to themselves and reassured Ted. "Let's just see how things work out," they told him.
>
> Surprisingly, Ted seemed to thrive on the work load. He saw it as a challenge and not a problem. He learned to

manage his time as he never had before. Being able to successfully complete the homework helped to underscore his sense of accomplishment as well as enhance his own self-image as a good student. The ogre had turned out to be something of a mentor.

If your child follows an older sibling, try to build on whatever positive relationship you've already established. If there has been conflict or friction because of a previous child's relationship with that teacher, try to wipe the slate clean by acknowledging past difficulties and expressing a desire to start again.

Introduce yourself to the teacher soon. It is in the child's best interest when teachers and parents connect early in the school year. This provides an opportunity for teachers to learn about particular problems or family situations that might affect a child. The sharing of such information will make the teacher's job easier in trying to meet everyone's needs. In addition, it is helpful for you and the teacher to have a visual image of one another. A quick introduction, particularly if you and the teacher have never met or if your child is in the younger grades, signals your interest in your child's schooling.

The following suggestions may be helpful:

1. If at all possible, squeeze in a quick hello within the first few weeks of school. A convenient time to make contact may be just before the bell rings and children enter the classroom. Or you may prefer to stop by at the end of the school day when the teacher may have a few extra minutes. Whatever time you decide to squeeze in your "hello," be careful not to interrupt a class or an activity. You also may simply introduce yourself with a brief note.

2. Be brief. Start with something like, "Hello, I'm Joy's father. I just wanted to let you know how much she is enjoying the class. Call me if I can be of any help to you." Such a first contact is more than enough. Since you haven't made a specific appointment, the teacher will not be prepared for a lengthy discussion about your child or

the academic agenda. Unless your child has special medical or other needs that you must inform the teacher about immediately, keep your introduction shorter than five minutes. "It's always awkward when parents come in and want to hang around to chat just as we're beginning to get settled for the day," comments a second-grade teacher. "I love to meet parents, but the timing has got to be right."

3. Try to acknowledge the teacher's effort to prepare a welcoming classroom. If you venture into the classroom, try to notice and comment on some aspect of the room that is especially appealing. Elementary school teachers understand that an attractive, inviting classroom creates a warm learning environment and helps children become comfortable with their new surroundings. Teachers work hard prior to the opening of school to prepare their rooms for their students. Noticing the bulletin board, posters, setup of the room, or other decorations will show you understand and appreciate the teacher's efforts. "I usually spend quite a bit of extra time before school opens to decorate my room," says a kindergarten teacher. "Throughout the summer I look for posters and other materials that will help liven up the bulletin boards. I cut out magazine pictures and think up themes for each subject area. I can sense when kids like my room, but when a parent mentions it I feel especially validated."

4. Assure the teacher that you are available. Teachers find it helpful when they are aware of families' receptiveness about sharing in what is happening at school as well as knowing the best way to reach them. A quick comment encouraging the teacher to be in touch with you—especially if there is a concern—that mentions how you can be contacted gives the teacher helpful information. In addition, you may want to let the teacher know your basic schedule. To keep your initial meeting brief, you may wish to jot down the information on an index card that you can give to the teacher.

Keeping the Relationship Going

A year is a long time. When opportunities arise, the following practices can help to continue strengthening your relationship with your child's teacher:

Respond promptly to questionnaires and notices that are sent home. Try to establish a habit of sending back permission slips, book club money, class picture forms, breakfast and/or lunch applications, school insurance forms, and so forth as soon as possible. Teachers know what a nuisance paperwork can be. Most forms are returned the next day and the rest tend to require repeated reminders. Your promptness will not only help a teacher's bookkeeping tasks but also will allow more time for teaching. A parent's reliable and responsible attitude as well as assistance in teaching this responsibility to children is greatly appreciated. On the other hand, try to respect your child's privacy and support the newly emerging sense of responsibility by resisting the urge to go through the school bag or backpack yourself.

One of the ways teachers get notices returned is to write names on the board of children who have not returned them. This helps to ensure that no one misses out on something important. Yet, even that doesn't always work. Here's an example of one possible result of unreturned paperwork: "The day I forgot to send back a signed permission slip about a field trip," remembers Marie Caldor, a parent, "was a disaster. My daughter actually had to stay back from going on a special, and very wonderful, Outward Bound program because neither I nor my husband could be reached before the busses left. After that, I made sure I never forgot another notice again!"

Expect to schedule a parent-teacher conference within the first several weeks of school. At the traditional back-to-school or open house night in the early fall, you will learn about what is happening in the classroom as well as have an opportunity to introduce yourself to the teacher. In particular, the teacher will share expectations concerning academic programs and ways families can support their children. Back-to-school-night also provides an opportunity for teachers to explain to families how they can best communicate with the teacher and the school during the year.

At this time you may be invited to sign up for a parent-teacher conference. If there isn't a convenient time listed on the sign-up sheet in the classroom, ask the teacher if there are other options. If you have more than one child in the school and you prefer to make one trip to school, mention to the teacher that you would like to schedule back-to-back conferences. Teachers are generally very accommodating.

And you don't have to wait for the teacher to arrange for a conference first. Whether or not you have a specific concern, you may wish to initiate the conference yourself. Maybe you'd like to share some overall insights about your child that may help the teacher get to know your child better. By requesting a conference you are helping to establish a pattern of working with the teacher toward mutual goals. (See guidelines for conferences later in this chapter.)

Give yourself credit!   Teachers bring professional knowledge and experience to their work but you can provide the teacher with special insights about your child. Sharing your perspective with your child's teachers is invaluable in assisting them (such as at a conference mentioned above) and working together.

It is particularly helpful to inform teachers if there is a change at home. While some children do not react to changes, others do. "I had a child in class who was very disruptive at the beginning of the year," says first-grade teacher Adrianne Ryder.

> When I met his mother I found out that his father's job had changed, causing him to commute long distances to work and leaving very little time for him to be with his son. Once I knew what was causing the change in the child's behavior I was not only able to show empathy but also to work out ways for him to express his fears and concerns about his father's difficult routine.

By sharing what you can with the teacher, you are giving the teacher the opportunity to best meet your child's needs.

Discuss concerns with the teacher directly and confidentially. There is a great deal of informal discussion among staff members during the day. When a classroom teacher finds out that you have talked about an issue that was assumed to be private, the trust that you have been building can be jeopardized. When you and the teacher speak, the trust between you will be enhanced if confidentiality is respected.

If possible, participate in a classroom activity or field trip. In the best of all worlds this sounds reasonable, yet with insufficient hours in the day to do what you must, even an hour or two to help out with a special assembly or classroom program may be unrealistic. However, anyone can help out. When Craig's mom couldn't drive on the field trip, his grandmother substituted. She had a great time, the children loved her, and Craig thought her presence was a special treat.

Further Tailoring the Relationship to Meet the Demands on Your Life

As the year progresses life often becomes more hectic and problematic rather than less so. Busy is a word that characterizes almost everyone. What do you do when

- the car dies and the teacher is expecting you?
- you've been out of work and a job interview is scheduled at the same time as your son's class play?
- the school informs you that your daughter is sick but there's no one available to pick her up at school?

It's no wonder that more and more often teachers hear "I'm overextended" or "My plate is full." Sound familiar? You're not alone. Just as you think you have things under control, unanticipated events can happen.

Yvette LaFontaine really liked her job. When her daughter Caroline started kindergarten, she was thrilled to no longer have to worry about baby-sitters and day care. But by

71

October, Ms. LaFontaine realized that school wasn't going to make her life easier. The introductory class picnic coincided with an important business meeting, and she was looking forward to meeting Caroline's teacher. In addition, she knew she couldn't chaperone the first two field trips and felt embarrassed sending store-bought cookies to the Halloween party. Now, instead of feeling guilty only when things got busy at the office and she had to stay late, she felt guilty just about all the time.

Fortunately, schools recognize that families have varying commitments and will demonstrate flexibility in meeting your changing needs.

One parent, having to juggle time for three children, used to try to do it all. Thinking back she said, "I must have been trying to prove something to my children, to the school, and to myself." As her children got older, she discovered that the school would still reach out to her children despite her limited time. While schools and families need to interact, there is no one keeping score or expecting you to do everything. (See Chapter 7 for information about volunteering.)

The following ideas will help you keep things in perspective so that you can continue to communicate effectively with your child's teacher.

You and the teacher may have a great deal in common. Many teachers—like you—have multiple responsibilities. In fact, teachers who wear many hats themselves can relate to your conflicting priorities.

Nevertheless, you may encounter a teacher who appears less than sympathetic to your needs. This teacher may seem unwilling to schedule an early or late parent-teacher conference or may expect you to be available as a room parent or helper in ways that don't work for you. The best thing you can do is to be kind but explicit. Don't feel that you need to apologize for your commitments. Rather, explain your work schedule or other responsibilities clearly and indicate any alterations you could make. You might say, "I'm really sorry that I can't make a conference at three-thirty. My boss is very strict about my taking off before five o'clock. But perhaps I could ask special permission to leave an hour early one day. Would four-thirty be manageable?" If teachers see that you are willing to make compromises in order to accommodate their needs also, they may be more willing to meet you halfway. Also, telling your child's teacher about your situation will give the teacher a picture of the reasons behind your level of involvement with other things that may arise.

On the other hand, try not to use your obligations as an excuse to avoid participating in school activities. Rather than dwell on what you can't do, let the teacher know what you can do instead. For instance, if other parents are coming in to talk about their family tree as part of a social studies unit, perhaps you could send in some family photographs. If you cannot be part of a phone chain about a school event because you have evening commitments, perhaps you can volunteer to send in refreshments for a special event.

If possible, offer to share your skills or interests with the class. Whatever your occupation, it's likely that children will find it interesting. Whether you are a fire fighter, postal worker, fast-food manager, computer technician, a medical worker, or work at home, let your child's teacher know if you are willing to talk with the class about it. If you wonder just how to go about preparing for a presentation, ask the teacher what would be of interest to the children or fit in with a unit of study. This will focus you and make your task easier. One parent was overheard saying, "I'd love to share how math is an important part of my work." Rest assured that the teacher will appreciate your offer to enrich the classroom.

Look to other parents for information about what is happening at school. There are always certain parents who seem to be more in the know than others. Don't hesitate to ask someone with whom you may have only a casual relationship to fill you in. If there is a meeting you can't attend, find someone you can contact after the meeting. Or if a friend has volunteered to go on a school trip, find out how things went.

The PTO provides a wonderful opportunity to connect with other families and learn about school issues. Attending even an occasional meeting provides you with information and gives you the opportunity to ask questions and hear what others have to say. (See Chapter 7 for information about the PTO.)

Attend whatever school events or activities you can. Appearing at school to see a class play or join a holiday celebration lets your child know you care. If you do make a commitment to come to a field trip or other special event, make every effort to follow through. Your child is likely to be disappointed if you are unable to attend.

If you absolutely cannot attend a performance, try to find out if it will be possible to see it at another time. In order to provide opportunities for all students to attend, many schools will schedule more than one performance or program. You may even be able to attend a rehearsal.

> Denise Ewing knew that she'd be out of town for the third-grade poetry recital. When she learned that there would be a dress rehearsal the day before, she was able to come by for an hour and see the show then. Her son was thrilled that his mother got a sneak preview and a special seat in the auditorium. In addition, the teacher and the principal noticed that Ms. Ewing was there. They were impressed by her special effort to attend. It not only sent a strong message of support to her child but made him feel more comfortable the next day when other families were there and his was not.

You might also find out through the principal or program director if the performance is being videotaped. Families often do this and may be willing to give you a copy or have you borrow theirs.

Using the Parent-Teacher Conference to Maximize the Relationship

At the same time that you are taking measures to stay on top of things and ensure a positive working relationship with your child's teacher, the school reaches out to promote and maintain good home-school communication as well. One of the ways schools do this is through the parent-teacher conference.

The following exchange took place between two friends whose children are in the same first-grade class.

> Parent #1: "Did you have your conference with Ms. Donnelley yet?"
>
> Parent #2: "I did. She seems very nice. But there was just one problem. With all that was said, I left the conference wondering, 'Just how is he doing?'"
>
> Parent #1: "I know how that feels. I, too, wish we had more time."

Is needing more time the answer? Conferences are one way to keep the channels of communication open. But there are times when the experience falls short of your expectations. Whether the conference is the only contact you have with the teacher all year or one of many contacts, it is the responsibility of both you and the teacher to make the conference successful.

Arrangements for conferences can vary. To accommodate the differing needs of families, conferences can be held on the telephone, at the workplace, at convenient public buildings, and at times of day other than regular business hours. The purpose of the conference and the role children have in the conference also differ. You may be asked to review an upcoming report card, to talk about overall progress, or to discuss a particular situation. In addition, in some schools, children become active participants. What remains relatively constant is that whatever the format of the conference, or whoever initiates it, the overall goal is generally the same: to discuss your child's school experience and learn about how he/she is progressing.

Teachers realize that to have productive conferences they need to communicate effectively. They are encouraged to

Avoid using educational jargon. Teachers should try to refrain from using shop talk when talking to families. When the terminology teachers use is easy to understand, the conference is more likely to be viewed as helpful.

Start and end conferences on a positive note. Everyone likes to hear good things. When conferences begin with, "What a wonderful smile he has" instead of "He baffles me," you feel drawn in rather than put off. By the same token, when a conference, even a difficult one, ends with, "We've covered a lot of important ground today," you will feel that everyone is working together.

Listen and learn from your perspective. To best understand your child, teachers would like you to share the way you see your child at home. This can provide valuable assistance in helping the child in school. Teachers need to hear comments such as, "Although you notice that she's withdrawn in class, at home she's rather outgoing."

Demonstrate your child's progress by showing you samples of completed work. Teachers try to share information objectively. Whether or not the child is present for the conference, examples of your child's work are usually shown to you. When the teacher demonstrates a difference between work completed between September and January, you can see for yourself how your child is progressing.

State their expectations for your child and explain what needs to be done to achieve them. By supportively saying to you, "Pasquale needs to read fifteen minutes in the evening and spend ten minutes going over his multiplication tables," you know exactly what the teacher recommends in order to assist your child. The teacher may further say, "If he does this each night for one month, you will have been a great help in encouraging him to master his facts and read more confidently."

Plan a follow-up conference if necessary. Teachers are encouraged to discuss the timing of the next meeting if there is to be one. A teacher may suggest, "Let's touch base in one month to see how things are going," or "Call me if you have any further concerns."

Time constraints or individual styles might prevent a teacher from following through on each of these suggestions consistently.

A teacher may deviate from some of these guidelines if you have spoken recently or if you are discussing an isolated situation other than in the context of a routine conference.

Below are some suggestions to help you ensure a productive conference:

Prepare for the conference ahead of time. By organizing your questions or concerns, you demonstrate that you are a true collaborator with the teacher. This provides you and the teacher with the best opportunity to focus on your child's needs and to determine together how they can be met.

Come to the conference with notes about your concerns and be ready to take notes, even if you are having a telephone conference. Bringing prepared notes to the conference enhances your ability to initiate your own questions and taking notes allows you to reflect on what the teacher has said. Although most teachers are supportive, if the teacher appears uncomfortable with the notes you bring, you might respond, "I know our time is limited and I don't want to forget anything." If the teacher is uncomfortable with notes you take, you could say, "This helps me recall what you have said so I can share your comments with my child."

Approach the conference free of distractions. If you're late for an another appointment or your child is waiting for you outside the classroom door, it may be difficult to concentrate on what the teacher is saying. If possible, encourage your child to use the library or computer lab while waiting for you. If child care is not available and you have younger children with you at the conference, provide them with something to do such as a coloring project or a game to play or ask them to begin their homework. This should make it easier to give your full attention to your conversation with the teacher.

Be aware of the time. If possible, plan to arrive a few minutes early. If a conference preceding yours finishes early or the teacher is free for some other reason, you may be asked to come in early, which might give you extra time for the conference. If the conference before yours is running late, try to be patient. The teacher probably is aware of this and knows that you are waiting.

In addition, realize that conference time flies. While it is important in building your relationship with the teacher to "break the ice" for a few minutes before you begin the substance of the conference, this takes time. Throughout the conference it is a good idea to be aware of the time so that both of you can have a sufficient opportunity to share your thoughts.

Ask for clarification. If the teacher says, "Mary is disrespectful," you might ask the teacher to elaborate by then asking, "What does she do that shows you she is disrespectful?" The teacher may then say, "Mary interrupts, she ridicules other students' work, and talks back." You now know exactly what to report to Mary. Even if the teacher says, "I wish I had a whole class of Marys," you can ask what the teacher means by that as well.

If your philosophies conflict, talk. If your thinking and that of the teacher coincide, it is easy to work together. But if you see issues differently you can reach an impasse. For example, at one parent-teacher conference a discussion about the value of giving letter grades for third-grade classwork came up. The parents believed that grades motivated children and felt their children needed them in order to do well. The teacher disagreed, saying that "Grades shouldn't matter. Children should want to learn for the sake of learning." After much discussion the teacher created a rating scale that would assess student's performance. The teacher and parents saw this as a compromise that could meet everyone's needs.

Speak with your child before you meet with the teacher. Your child should know you are going to meet with the teacher even if not formally included in the conference. Before you leave for the conference, you might ask, "Is there anything you would you like me to discuss with the teacher?" Even if your child offers nothing, if it is appropriate, report what the teacher and you discussed, sharing your child's successes as well as areas for improvement.

Ask the teacher what you can do to help your child at home. This is another expression of your willingness to work in partner-

78

ship with the school. If the suggestions are workable for you, the teacher will expect you to follow through. If they are not, let the teacher know. You may need to say something such as, "Weekday evenings are difficult, but I can help her review on weekends when I have more time."

If time has run out and issues still need to be resolved, ask the teacher if you can meet again to finish. If you feel that you are left hanging, be open about it. You could say to the teacher, "This has been helpful, but there are still areas that we need to address. Could we schedule another meeting shortly?"

Review what transpired. Before you leave you might say, "The way I understand it, you think Jack should read by himself before bed every night as well as be read to each night. May we speak again in one month about how things are going?"

Should Your Child Be Present at the Conference?

There are pros and cons to having children participate in conferences. Some parents and teachers find it helpful to include students at conferences, yet others find it problematic. Some teachers routinely include children in conferences, some do occasionally, some invite children to be present during part of the conference, and some never include children at all.

If you wish your child's teacher to change the structure being used for your conferences, share your thoughts with the teacher.

- To have a conference just between you and the teacher, you might say at the time the appointment is arranged that, "There are some things I would like to discuss with you privately. May the two of us meet alone this time?" Most teachers will provide an opportunity for you to do this.
- You may want to have your child included in the conference. Appearing at the classroom door with your child at your side, saying, "I hope you don't mind if I brought Lucy," gets Lucy to the meeting, but it takes the teacher by surprise. Instead, plan ahead. Find out how the teacher

feels about the child coming to the conference at the time the appointment for the conference is made. Ask your child as well. Each may have concerns that you did not anticipate. Also, teachers prepare for conferences in advance, and their approach to the conference may be different if a child is going to be present.

- If you wish to have your child included during part of the conference, discuss this with the teacher and your child ahead of time, as well.

A productive parent-teacher conference will be of ultimate benefit to your child. Use the conference as an opportunity to share, to listen, and to learn.

It's the Little Things That Count

Successful parent-teacher relationships are based not only on teachers recognizing the needs of parents but also on parents acknowledging the needs of teachers. One way of doing this is to express appreciation for their efforts.

The following example illustrates one parent who demonstrates appreciation and another who does not.

Jeff and George, two students in Mr. Minton's sixth-grade math class need extra help. Their test scores in math are low, even though they both do their homework. Mr. Minton has asked the students to stay after school several times to work with them each individually.

Jeff's mother called Mr. Minton to say how much she appreciated his efforts even though Jeff was still having problems improving. George's mother, however, has said nothing, not even when she sees Mr. Minton for another purpose.

This scenario suggests that Mr. Minton's needs might have been more adequately met by Jeff's mother, who showed appreciation, than by George's mother, who didn't.

In looking at needs more closely it may be helpful to understand some of the work of the noted psychologist Abraham Maslow, who differentiated among basic human needs. [1] According to Maslow, needs range in a hierarchy. He suggested that lower-level needs must be met before higher-level needs. Examples of some lower-level needs of teachers might include an adequate salary, job security, or a safe and comfortable work environment. Higher-level needs may include being appreciated by the school community or experiencing a sense of satisfaction from giving the best effort, or watching students grow. Maslow said that when all needs are met a person is said to be "self-actualized" or completely fulfilled.

Of course, teachers should ideally perform their jobs equally and adequately with each child. But teachers are not machines. The extent to which their needs are being met can influence their job performance. When families recognize and appreciate a teacher's hard work, they help reenergize and sustain a teacher's commitment. No one else, not even the principal, can give the kind of positive feedback a parent can give to the teacher. Your perspective is unique since you are able to best observe and appreciate your child's progress.

During your child's school career, there are many opportunities for you to show appreciation to teachers. They may include situations when a teacher has

- helped your child through a particularly sensitive personal issue,
- responded to a need for extra help in order to support your child's learning,
- followed through during a crisis,
- supported you during a difficult time,
- used a particularly creative or effective approach to help your child grow,
- volunteered to lead an extra school activity or take over other duties in order to fill a gap or need—thus giving your child an opportunity to participate, or
- achieved professional recognition.

Perhaps you have encountered one or more of these situations. Understandably, while devoting all your energy to your child's needs you may have forgotten to show your appreciation. It is never too late to remedy this. The simplest thank you is highly valued.

In addition to thanking a teacher for a particular effort at any time, many families like to show their appreciation to teachers near holidays or at the end of the school year. Despite the existence of no gift policies in some communities, you may have observed teacher's desks piled high with beautifully wrapped presents of all sizes and shapes. Contrary to what you may see, many teachers, whether or not the school permits it, prefer that you do not give them personal gifts. In addition to possibly creating competition among families to see who can give the teacher the nicest or most lavish gift, gift giving also puts pressure on the family who can't afford a gift or who just doesn't believe in giving teachers gifts. This can become awkward for the teacher and embarrassing for the student.

Consider the following:

Write a thank-you note. Sending a note is one of the simplest ways to express your appreciation. Rather than offering a broad comment such as "Karen is happier about coming to gym class," try to be specific: "By helping Karen overcome her fear of climbing the ropes, she now looks forward to being first to the top!" Teachers love to hear not just that they are doing a good job, but exactly how their efforts are working for your child.

Thank-you notes are also appropriate when the results are not quite as satisfactory or the process changes, as in the following example:

> Mr. Jackson, a second-grade teacher, had worked tirelessly with Desmond in class to improve his reading comprehension. Despite Mr. Jackson's best efforts, Desmond still was having trouble and required the specialized attention of a tutor three days a week. Tutoring achieved the goal of improving his comprehension skills. Desmond's mother wrote to thank Mr. Jackson for his extra help and sensitivity in recognizing Desmond's needs even though the support of the tutor was something that she had not originally anticipated.

Use casual opportunities to say thank you.   If you happen to be speaking to the teacher about another matter or you meet your child's teacher unexpectedly, it only takes a few seconds to express a quick thank you. You might mention that "Carl really enjoyed your science lesson yesterday. Thanks for an exciting day!" You can use an informal meeting to let the teacher know you have appreciated a well-planned lesson, a creative homework assignment, or a fun class project.

If you can't get to school, appreciation can still be expressed on paper. One way to do this is to write a comment on one of your child's papers that needs to be returned with your signature. Knowing how uncomfortable children sometimes feel when families write anything to the teacher, you may want to share what you plan to write with your child first. It only takes a few seconds to add a *P.S.* to the signed paper.

The following suggestions can be carried out by individuals, an entire class, or the whole school. Because they benefit many they are usually very well received.

Donate a book to the school library in the name of the teacher.   Some schools suggest this idea as an alternative to personal gifts. If the school doesn't have a library donation system in place, you can call the school librarian and mention that you would like to give a book in the name of your child's teacher(s). The librarian will tell you what the library needs, suggest how you might proceed, and inform the teacher of your gift. In the absence of a school librarian, you might contact a room parent or PTO president for guidance. To reduce the cost or express a shared appreciation, you may also want to donate a book with another family. Names of the donors are often pasted in the book on a decorative book plate.

Purchase a magazine subscription for a class or donate a classroom gift.   This is best accomplished by consulting with your child or the teacher first rather than making a specific choice on your own. This could place you in the uncomfortable position of asking the teacher to accept something that is inappropriate, as occurred in the following situation:

Greg Stevens wanted to do something special for his son's fourth-grade science teacher. He decided to give a subscription to a scientific magazine to the class but didn't realize, however, that the magazine was far too challenging in content and reading level for the class. If he had spoken to the teacher ahead of time he could have ordered a more suitable one.

Make a small donation to a cause the class or teacher supports. It may be easiest to ask the teacher for the name of the charity or organization such as a homeless shelter, soup kitchen, or senior citizens center, and mention what you would like to do.

If you can contact the organization by letter, enclose a note with your check stating that the donation is in honor of a given teacher and that you would like an acknowledgment to be sent to that person. List the school's address.

As in any demonstration of teacher appreciation, it is the thought, not the amount of the donation that counts. In fact, most organizations will not state the amount you gave when they contact the teacher. What's most important is that the teacher will know that you took the time to do something that was meaningful.

Help organize a gift of children's work to present to the teacher. An entire class can become involved in writing a poem, story, or collecting individual pictures or writings to give to the teacher. If each child writes an essay on "What We Will Remember About Ms. Powell" or "What I Liked About Second Grade," the result can be a valuable compilation that Ms. Powell will always treasure.

Sometimes planned as an end-of-the-year treat, this can be a memorable way to recognize a teacher. Very often children can organize this event themselves, with the guidance of families or with a student teacher. When initiated by students, teachers thoroughly appreciate not only the project itself but the students' ability to organize themselves—and keep a secret!

Carol Peterson, the music teacher, had spent the first part of the year familiarizing the children with ballads and acquainting them with familiar composers of ballads. As a treat, several of her students got together and composed their own ballad about Ms. Peterson. They sang it to her during a winter concert. Ms. Peterson valued this unique tribute because it was personal and heartfelt. To her delight, it also demonstrated that she had done her job well—the children had really learned about ballads.

A group presentation gives a teacher a terrific sense of accomplishment. Teachers take pride in how far their students have come during the year.

Write a note to the principal and send a copy to the teacher. If you feel strongly about showing support for a teacher, sending a note to the principal is also an option. With so much occurring in a school simultaneously, principals may be unaware of a teacher's special efforts for a child. Again, if the note focuses on a particular situation, try to be specific in expressing exactly what the teacher did or said. Families often forget to let principals know how they feel—except when there's a crisis. Communicating with the principal about something positive is always welcome. (See Chapter 6 for guidelines on communicating with the principal.)

Andrew was absent from school for over a week with chicken pox. Sara Hurley, his fifth-grade teacher, decided that the best way for Andrew to keep up would be to hear explanations about the homework directly from her rather than get them from another student. So each day she sent him a tape of her voice explaining the assignments. This was clearly an extra and very thoughtful effort. Ms. Hurley didn't think to mention her solution to the principal. But Andrew's mother was very impressed and wrote a note to the principal explaining how helpful the tapes had been. The principal congratulated Ms. Hurley on her creativity.

Hold a teacher appreciation day. This might result in a schoolwide undertaking. Often organized by the PTO, it involves many participants and can have a positive impact on the entire school community. Whether you choose to have a breakfast, luncheon, or other expression of appreciation, it is important to check with the principal in advance.

Showing appreciation can take many forms. By recognizing teachers, you help to strengthen the parent-teacher bond. Being appreciated by families is the icing on the cake that encourages teachers to reach above and beyond their role. Whatever way you choose to show your appreciation is worthwhile.

Conclusion

All relationships need to be nurtured. The relationship you and your child's teacher establish requires mutual sensitivity and a willingness to express your needs to the teacher as well as learn the teacher's expectations of you and your child. Establishing a trusting, collaborative relationship at the beginning of the year that can be built upon as the year progresses is relatively easy when one considers the benefits to all concerned!

Notes
1. Abraham Maslow, *Motivation and Personality*, New York: Harper and Row, 1970.

Chapter 5

Addressing Problems: Approaching the Teacher and Keeping Your Cool

Think Before You Act

The following situation describes a mother's account of her family's frustration.

> Our entire family had begun to dread evenings. Almost as soon as Mark had gone into his room to do his homework, he would come out acting belligerent and demanding help. The assignments, especially in math, had become so challenging that no one, not even our older daughter, could figure out how to approach the work. Because this unhappiness had been occurring for weeks, we tried to get things straightened out. Mark spoke to the teacher on his own, which seemed to do no good, although she did say something to him about the importance of giving challenging homework assignments.
>
> Continuing to be unable to complete the assignments and not even sure of what questions to ask the teacher, Mark went to school each day thinking, "I'm a failure and so is my family."
>
> Our family was angry at what seemed to be unfair assignments. We resented the pressure we were under, and I decided to give the teacher a piece of my mind. What was happening just didn't seem right!

This is a complex situation. What are the issues here? Did other families react in the same way? Should the teacher be doing something differently? Is there some information missing? Where do you begin to look for answers? A circumstance such as this demands your attention. The pressure is on you to do something.

The mother did vent her frustration at the teacher, which resulted in some changes that were made at home and at school. But this was not without a painful exchange that the parent and the teacher regretted.

It is sometimes difficult to maintain your objectivity—and your positive relationship with the teacher—while trying to sort out a problem. Your emotional involvement may interfere with your ability to look at the facts, understand the situation, and effectively communicate your feelings as you work your way to the bottom of the issue. It is easy to say things during a highly charged discussion, but remember that statements made in the heat of the moment can't be retracted. Be a good listener and consider the approach of Dr. Haim Ginott, child psychotherapist: avoid taking sides and focus on solving the problem. This will bring you to a resolution more quickly and more productively. [1]

In the case above, the problem came to the attention of the family because of Mark's reaction to the homework. If the teacher had realized—and perhaps the only way she could was if Mark's family had told her what effect these assignments were having on Mark and his household—she would have considered finding ways to assist Mark in class or possibly modifying the assignments for everyone.

What follows is another situation requiring attention:

> Deborah's mother noticed that her daughter had not been interacting with her friends as often as usual. Deborah had also become critical of family members and was difficult to be with at home. At the same time, her teacher had noticed a change in her schoolwork. Assignments were completed haphazardly, which was different from Deborah's normal pattern of doing her work carefully.

When Deborah's schoolwork indicated to the teacher that something could be wrong, she contacted the family. The family, also sensing a problem, first spoke with their daughter and included her in a meeting with the teacher. It was discovered that Deborah had had a falling out with her best friend and was probably reacting to it. A strategy for solving Deborah's problem with her friend would be tried and it was hoped that when that issue was resolved her schoolwork would improve. The teacher, Deborah's parents, and Deborah would talk again soon to review the situation.

Not all problems or concerns will be called to your attention by the school, nor will you notice them all yourself. While you may not be looking for problems, it's important to be alert and aware of the possibility that they may exist.

So how do you know when you have a problem on your hands? It is often your child who will tell you. While your child may explain the problem clearly, it is also possible that it will be discovered through a clue. Here are some examples:

- *behavior changes:* A child refuses to do homework, plays sick, comes home crying for seemingly innocuous reasons, or overreacts to simple requests at home.
- *complaints from the child:* A child says, "No one likes me," "I don't want to go to gym any more," "The teacher is mean," or "I was sent to the office and it wasn't my fault."
- *stories:* If a child comes home with a story that sounds outrageous to you, don't dismiss it entirely—it may contain seeds of truth.
- *physical changes:* A child complains about stomachaches or headaches or loses appetite and a physician has ruled out physical causes.

Before acting or reacting—regardless of whether the concern originates with the school, your child, or yourself—take a step back and consider three questions as you speak with your child:

1. Can I resolve this with my child at home? Is this simpler than it sounds?
2. Can I help my child resolve this at school with the teacher or can I work it out with the teacher myself?

3. Will this potentially require the involvement of other professionals?

Ask your child if there is anything important for you to know. Often a child will come right out with enough information so that together you can resolve the difficulty and keep from making a mountain out of something simple. It also encourages you and your child to solve problems in a way that teaches your child responsibility and promotes self-confidence. By continuing to ask questions, you can help clarify your child's thinking and determine the appropriate level of your involvement.

However, getting your child to approach a problem with you or independently with the teacher is not always practical or appropriate. The approach you use will be determined by the problem and the individual style of everyone involved, including that of your child.

The following discussion is focused primarily on concerns involving parents approaching the teacher. It should help you understand some sources of difficulties and provide you with guidelines for communicating with the teacher.

Unless the problem is of crisis magnitude, let the situation cool down. Your first instinct may be to jump right in, but it may be best to let a day or two pass. What can seem earth-shattering one day may lose its urgency the next. If you and your child are still concerned, contact the teacher.

By trying to assess the seriousness of the problem first, you can discriminate between those issues that would benefit from your involvement and those issues that wouldn't. Consider the following two situations:

Upon returning a test to a second-grade class, the teacher said, "I thought you people were smarter than this. Where are your brains? You can't possibly be thinking!" When Libby got home that day she was upset and told her mother what the teacher said.

Paul told his mother that "My teacher is picking on me. His mother said, "What do you mean? Paul responded, "Every day Mr. Robbins calls me up to his desk and makes me read out loud for him." Paul continued to report for several days that the teacher was still picking on him. Just as Paul's mother was about to call the teacher, Paul came home and announced happily, "Guess what? Mr. Robbins was just giving me extra attention in reading so that by next week I'll be ready to move on to the next book with the rest of my friends."

In the first situation it is entirely appropriate for the parent to be concerned. Clearly the teacher's approach seems questionable. However, in the second situation, if Paul's mother hadn't waited a few days she might have jumped into a situation that didn't require her involvement. Paul solved the problem himself when he realized why he was getting the extra attention. Ultimately, Paul ended up liking his teacher more than ever.

Teaching practices, inadvertent mistakes, misunderstandings, educational philosophies, and school policies can become sources of conflict among families, school staff, and students. When your expectations clash with what seems to be occurring and you are dissatisfied, you must decide how, if, and when it is right for you to become involved.

What follows is an example of a teacher's practice causing a problem:

After several weeks of school, Ms. McNeil approached Susan Warwick, an eighth grader and a mediocre student. She said, "As you know, I was a great fan of your sister. Whenever she didn't understand something, she made sure to ask me to explain it and would come on her own for after-school help. I've written on your first two stories that you need to rewrite them with better organization, and I thought I would see you after school as I do many other students. I'd like you to come for extra help the way your sister always did. I'd rather not have to remind you to come."

Susan thought, "I always hear about how wonderful my sister is. Besides, I don't want extra help. Can't I be allowed to just be me?"

Ms. McNeil may not have realized that comparing Susan to her sister was lessening her interest in coming after school. The teacher's practice of expecting students to come on their own would not work for Susan.

Some teachers can't resist the temptation to make the same connection to siblings that Ms. McNeil did. Perhaps she thought that by bringing up the sister's name Susan would be more comfortable getting extra help. Unfortunately, comparing the sisters only made Susan feel demoralized.

Families often are unaware of teachers who compare one sibling to another. In this case, Susan was upset enough to let her family know how she felt. The family could have gone to see the teacher but instead decided to handle things at home with Susan, including letting her know how valued she was and that the teacher meant no harm.

If you fear sibling comparisons might affect your child, you can discourage them before they become a problem. You might mention to the teacher, perhaps at a conference that "I remember when you had our oldest son in class. He had a wonderful year. His younger sister, who is now in your class, is a different type of student. We are working at home toward helping her feel good about her successes rather than her brother's. Could you please support us by avoiding comparisons between them?"

Here is an illustration of a parent questioning a teacher's educational philosophy:

Patricia Fenwick, the mother of a second grader and a relatively new parent to the school, questioned whether her daughter was learning anything in school.

Wanting to do everything right, she waited for the teacher to get to know the class before getting involved. But when she realized that the classroom did not use a reading book with its own workbook such as she had used as a student, Ms. Fenwick decided this alone confirmed her concerns that her child was not being sufficiently challenged. Ms. Fenwick accused the teacher of using inappropriate teaching materials. This approach created uneasiness between the two of them.

Although the teacher welcomed communication with families, the mother lacked the confidence to know how

92

to find out why the reading program was different from her expectations without jeopardizing the parent-teacher relationship.

Ms. Fenwick needed information. After receiving answers to questions such as "How is reading taught?" "What books are used?" "Why choose one approach rather than another?" or "How can one tell if the children are being sufficiently challenged?" she would have become better informed. Then, if she didn't agree with the teacher about the reading program, she could voice her ultimate concerns about the overall level of challenge in the classroom.

Receiving answers to your questions may not convince you that a particular philosophy or approach is best for your child, but it will make you more aware of what is happening in the classroom and the reasons for it. If you are still concerned after speaking to the teacher, you may wish to discuss the matter with another staff member or the principal. (See Chapters 3 and 6.)

Parents can be misled by their children's comments. The following parent regretted his reaction.

> George Dean was helping his second-grade son, Christopher, get ready for bed. Although George had worked late that evening, he was glad that he had a chance to spend a few minutes with his son before bedtime.
>
> Just as Christopher was about to brush his teeth, George asked, "So Chris, what did you do in school today?"
>
> Christopher replied, "Dad, today was the best. My friends and I spent all morning in the corridors!"
>
> "What do you mean?" questioned George.
>
> "During math, Ms. Lopez told us we could go wherever we wanted as long as we weren't too noisy."

Mr. Dean thought, "This is no way to teach math. When I went to school students never would have been allowed to do that. Not only will I speak to the teacher about Chris, but I will also speak up for the other parents, who I'm sure would feel the same way."

Mr. Dean did this. However in the course of his discussion with the teacher he learned the whole story, which his son had not told him. This caused Mr. Dean to feel ridiculous and embarrassed, which resulted in an apology to the teacher. In truth, Ms. Lopez had sent the class to take measurements of actual spaces and objects in the school to reinforce their classroom study of measurement, which was a positive learning experience.

By jumping to conclusions Mr. Dean mishandled the situation. Had he asked more questions of his son or assumed that there was more information to be learned when speaking with the teacher, he could have prevented what happened. On the positive side, this confrontation gave the teacher a chance to share with Mr. Dean other math projects she planned, which he grew to support and appreciate. In addition, the teacher realized that more communication with families was needed.

Who Is Right?

If you decide to address a concern with a teacher or other staff member, you may learn that there are not always right or wrong answers. However, it's important to explore together and engage in dialogue.

Ms. Wheatley, a fourth-grade social studies teacher, wanted her class to learn the fifty states and their capitals. In the past she gave her students an alphabetical list to memorize. At the end of four weeks she gave them a test.

But lately, she had decided to build on her goal and develop a hands-on approach that would enable the children to do more than rattle off the list. She had the class make a giant puzzle map of the United States. By cutting out states, locating and labeling capitals, color-coding climates, making three-dimensional crops, and finding pictures of industry, her students would learn the states and their capitals and have a deeper understanding of each state's unique characteristics.

Erik's mother had no way of knowing that Ms. Wheatley was giving the students an opportunity to learn much more than the names of the states and their capitals. Because Erik wasn't learning this at the rate his mother thought he should or the way she learned them as a child, she questioned the teacher.

Who was right? The answer lies in perceptions. Each child, parent, and teacher is apt to look at any situation differently. What counts is everyone calmly looking at whatever the issue is and trying to understand other perceptions.

Again, talking things out with the teacher is the best way to see both points of view. Challenging a teacher's methodology is not easy. But when you look at classroom practices together, you might become aware of what the teacher is working to accomplish and develop increased respect for this person as a professional. You may be surprised to hear yourself thinking, "I wish I had been taught differently."

> It was the first report card of the year. The teacher was waiting for the report cards to be returned, signed with parents' comments. One parent made an appointment with the teacher to discuss the report card. She calmly said, "I know you would want me to ask this." She then questioned why her daughter's grades were so low in reading and writing skills. As the teacher looked over the grades she realized she had not been accurate, given the performance of the student. She explained, "I did her report card first. You're right. I think I graded her harder than the rest of the class." The teacher then thought to herself, "The grades were not justified." The teacher thanked the parent for her courage to bring it up and changed the grades to more accurately reflect the work of the student.

It was a simple mistake. The teacher didn't make excuses for the error but handled it graciously and gained the respect of the parent.

A Closer Look at How Teachers React

Have you ever wondered whether a teacher's approach to a child is affected by a parent's behavior? Will a teacher take frustration with a parent out on a child or reach out more as a result of what a parent does or says? While it is inappropriate and unprofessional for a teacher to deliberately vent dissatisfaction with a parent on a child by giving extra work or punishing the child in some other way, you still might question whether subtle reactions will occur as a result of what you might do or say.

No one should expect families to handle every concern perfectly. Even if your requests seem demanding or unreasonable, this is not an indication there will be negative repercussions for your child. The vast majority of teachers will continue to provide sound learning experiences to children regardless of their feelings about the parents of those children.

Yet teachers' reactions can vary, particularly if their professionalism is challenged. It's one thing to move a child's seat or change an approach with a child, but teachers may balk at parents who repeatedly advise them about what to teach and how to teach it. As one teacher said, "We are in public service positions, but we also have human sensitivities."

Teachers can react defensively to what they perceive as chronically unhappy parents. They may think, "I just can't seem to do anything right in this parent's eyes," and could be tempted to stop short of going out of their way for a child. The following teacher did just that.

Fourth-grade teacher Jackie Winston received a message to return a call from Joanne Carlson's mother. At the end of the school day, when Ms. Winston returned the call, Ms. Carlson said, "You know, Ms. Winston, I think it would be best for Joanne if you were to call on her only when she raises her hand. She's very shy and is really anxious when you call on her spontaneously."

"Fine," agreed Ms. Winston. "I'll be happy to do that."

A few days later there was another phone call. "I've been thinking," Ms. Carlson said, "If you don't mind, would you please allow Joanne to begin her homework during the last few minutes of class so she can let you know if she's having difficulty."

"I usually have students do that anyway." said Ms. Winston. "I'll check to see how she's doing."

96

At Joanne's routine conference two weeks later, Ms. Carlson suggested that Joanne didn't like to work in groups and she should be allowed to complete her project individually. Ms. Carlson also questioned the necessity of assigning the project at all.

Although all of the mother's requests had been expressed politely and respectfully, Ms. Winston had had enough. She thought to herself, "This parent is constantly pestering me for this, that, or the other thing." Ms. Winston decided that from now on she would do only what she had to for Joanne. She no longer felt motivated to reach out to the student or the parent.

Was Ms. Winston's reaction justified? Perhaps not. But when she felt that Ms. Carlson had established a habit of making teaching suggestions she felt undermined as a professional and somewhat manipulated. She probably wouldn't have considered one or two requests by Ms. Carlson excessive. However, when she felt a pattern was emerging, calling into question her own competence in managing her classroom, she began to resent the interference.

If you think you are establishing a habit of making continuous requests, discuss it with the teacher. The teacher may agree that there have been many requests while appreciating the importance of your open and honest input. If this happens, you can then reach out to the teacher asking, "How can we work on this together?" Rather than causing resentment, you are encouraging collaboration. This scenario is an extreme instance where a parent's response triggered a reaction in the teacher:

Ms. Brown took great pains and a lot of time to correct essay tests. She raised thought-provoking issues in her comments and paid strict attention to proper grammar and spelling. Jonathan's parents, however, began to see more red ink than blue on his papers and thought Ms. Brown's comments were confusing, excessive, and demoralizing. After repeatedly being questioned and challenged about the necessity of such detailed corrections, Ms. Brown gradually stopped working hard on Jonathan's behalf. She said to herself, "Why should I bother? His parents don't appreciate the time and effort I put into these things. Jonathan may not improve as much over the year, but at least his parents will leave me alone!"

Jonathan's parents could have participated in solving this problem by approaching the teacher for clarification of the corrections, as well as letting the teacher know if Jonathan felt badly about having many markings on his paper.

Your comments to the teacher can also obviously lead to helpful resolutions. In fact, a teacher may pay more attention to a child as a result of a parental request. One parent said to a teacher, "This may seem trivial, but right now friends are very important to Carlos. Sitting with certain friends motivates him to do his best work. Would you please observe him to see if you agree, and if necessary, adjust his seat accordingly? Would you let me know how things are going?" The teacher welcomed the parent's observation and happily accommodated the request.

When your actions affect an outcome in a positive manner, you have achieved your goal. If your actions, however, exacerbate a difficult situation by increasing tension and conflict, you have not only failed to reach your goal but have created a new set of problems. Before you act, try to anticipate whether there might be any consequences and adjust your intervention accordingly. We suggest keeping in mind the following points:

Encourage your children to take responsibility. If your child can ask for assistance for having a seat moved or getting extra help, you need not be involved beyond the support you give at home. Additionally, self-help encourages independence.

Pick your issues. By considering how important your concern is to your child's well-being before getting involved, you may decide that some issues will either take care of themselves or are best left alone. There are times when the best decision is to do nothing. You may even wish to consolidate several small concerns into one appointment with the teacher.

Keep a record of the times you contact the school and the issues you've addressed. Although this may seem tedious or unnecessary, it can be very useful. Each time you contact the school about a concern, write down the date of your call, the reason, and the decisions that were reached. You may forget or not realize how often you have chosen to intercede. For example, if you look at your list in November and you have approached the teacher six or seven times already about different concerns, you may need to reevaluate your effectiveness and decide it's time to change gears.

Be confident. You know your child best. Many of your interventions may reflect your need to tell the teacher something not previously known or understood about your child or to ask the school to help you identify what the problem is. If you feel it is important, speak to the teacher.

Achieve a reputation as a helpful parent. Express your concerns discreetly, focus on the issues, and speak in an honest but tactful manner. The teacher and school staff will come to welcome your comments. You will be regarded as a parent who expects accountability and communication and who can work with the school personnel in the best interests of your child. This reputation—based on the relationship you've already established with your child's teacher—will be your most important tool in dealing with day-to-day issues.

In the event you think something is being held against your child, address it. Speak with the teacher and explain what you think is happening as well as how your child feels about it. Use this meeting to share differences in perception. If you are still uncomfortable afterward, arrange a meeting with the principal. (See Chapter 6 for guidelines on meeting with the principal.)

Homework

Just as issues at school can generate concerns requiring communication with your child's teacher, homework issues such as the one described in this chapter's opening scenario may need your involvement as well. By considering some information about homework together with suggestions for resolving homework issues, you will be prepared to address concerns if it becomes necessary.

The following parent and child are stuck. This note was written directly on a homework assignment:

9:30 P.M.

Dear Mr. Bradley,

Donna has been working for one hour on these three math problems. She thought she understood your explanation in class but has not been able to do the homework. I didn't want her to stay up any later working on them.

Please do not be upset with her.

Sincerely,
Jim Whitehead

How would you feel if you were the teacher, parent, or student in this situation? Everyone has a different opinion about what homework should be, including the degree to which families should be involved. The most positive thing families can do is to have a supportive attitude and share concerns with the teacher.

Why Is Homework Given?

Your child's teacher may assign homework to

- reinforce, follow-up, or review material introduced in class,
- apply outside of class (usually at home) something that was learned at school,
- promote independent thinking and effective study habits,
- develop responsibility for completing tasks efficiently, and/or
- practice interpreting directions.

It may be helpful to note that in giving any homework assignment the teacher often has more than one purpose in mind. An assignment may include objectives that refer to the content, or work itself, and it may also have objectives related to the process of doing the homework. For example, writing a report on Egypt involves more than learning about Egypt. It may require going to the library, using the card catalog or computer, taking notes, writing a draft, proofreading, and presenting a report. The purpose of the assignment becomes twofold: learning facts about Egypt is a content goal, and practicing the procedures in gathering information is a process goal.

Doing Homework Isn't Always Smooth Sailing

While it would be nice to imagine all children tackling their homework successfully and cheerfully, there are times when you may observe frustration, which sometimes leads to tears. Perhaps some of these situations have occurred in your household.

- Your child complains of too much work.
- Your child complains of work being too difficult.
- You realize that your child needs to go to bed but is still working.
- Your child is unclear about what to do, and you don't understand the assignment either.
- There is homework assigned on a night that your child has an unexpected obligation and the work cannot be completed.
- You would like to help your child, but you have no time.

Any of these situations could result in unpleasantness at home, which may cause you to unintentionally make the situation worse. We suggest that you try to avoid expressing sentiments to your child such as:

"I'm going to tell her a thing or two. Don't you worry, Johnny. I'll take care of everything."

"Your teacher has no business asking you to do this for homework!"

"When I was in school, no one helped me with my homework. Now it's your turn!"

You will also not be helping your child in the long run if you advise your child not to do the work (or not to worry about doing it), accuse your child of not paying enough attention or of misunderstanding the assignment, or do the work yourself.

By speaking against the teacher or advising children inappropriately, they can become confused and ambivalent about their loyalties to you and the teacher and find themselves in the position of having to take sides. One child thought, "I look up to my teacher in school. Now my parents are telling me that they don't think my teacher is doing the right thing. If my teacher finds out that my parents are mad at her, maybe she won't like me anymore."

Some Pointers

While some children will encourage their parents to intervene on their behalf, others may be uncomfortable with their involvement. Wanting to be independent and avoid having others enter their "space," children may also worry that the teacher will be upset with them or their family for their interfering.

Although teachers encourage children to be responsible for their homework, on occasion parents may still need to step in. Here are some suggestions about what you can do that should be comfortable for everyone:

Find out about the teacher's general expectations and philosophy of homework.   The best time to learn about this is at back-to-school-night, at a parent-teacher conference, or through a classroom newsletter. One teacher said, "Homework should be an extension of school. It is a time for children to practice on their own what they do at school. But it is not unusual for them to forget what to do when they get home."

Teachers will often tell you just how they would like you to assist your child. For instance, if your child is having difficulty you can ask, "What part is giving you trouble?" or "Tell me what you already know about this." Such an approach allows the child to take responsibility for the work. Teachers may suggest that children call a friend for assistance or that they give the assignment fifteen minutes and then bring it back to school. This could mean that a child will return a paper with no work completed or be encouraged to write a note at the top explaining what effort has been made.

Define your role in assisting your child. Most teachers will agree that families should view themselves as resources for their children. This view suggests that you should be available to encourage your children, help them focus or provide them with other forms of support but also that you insist that they be responsible for their own work. If you have limited time to be a resource, try to anticipate with your child whether you might be needed. By asking your child about homework, you might be able to plan to be available and avoid the surprise of the panic cry for support.

If you can't be in the house or in the room, try to be available when children begin their homework, even if it means a phone call to them if you are working late. Getting down to work can be just as difficult for children as it is for adults. Often they can't get past the directions, but once they do, it's clear sailing.

Children's calls for help may indicate that they are feeling isolated while working alone and may just need to have someone close by while completing their work. It is often sufficient if you can do your own work—and convey support by being available.

Encourage your child to take responsibility by speaking to the teacher about homework concerns directly. If you can encourage your child to talk to the teacher and explain the frustration, you have been effective in promoting self-assurance and independence. The teacher may clarify a question, suggest that your child join a before- or after-school homework club, or recommend doing homework with another child as a homework buddy. Your role as a resource is then reinforced, you remain on the sidelines and your involvement becomes secondary rather than primary. Everybody wins.

With your child's input, write a brief note explaining your concern. This can be done on the homework paper itself. If you think that the directions were confusing or the work took too long to complete, write just that. State how the assignment affected your child: "Daniel worked on this for an hour and then I insisted that he do his other work." When teachers receive notes like, "You should never have given an assignment that would take so long!" or "How do you expect the children to understand those directions? I couldn't even understand them!" they often feel defensive. Be sensitive to your child's feelings about what you write; review it together to be sure your child is comfortable.

Contact the teacher on your own to express your concern. This approach allows you to share issues of a more general nature such as "My son does the homework in five minutes. What's the point?" or "I see that she is consistently frustrated by the homework. Do you think expectations for her work should be changed?" Teachers often want to know if the homework is too long, short, easy, or difficult. Receiving such feedback helps teachers give better homework.

While this approach may address overall homework concerns, it may not solve your child's immediate problem. However, two-way communication between you and the teacher helps you avoid homework stress in your household and ensure productive homework experiences for your child.

Timing is important. Regardless of the homework concern, if a child is frustrated and worried about facing the teacher the next day, the assurance that you will address the issue next week provides little comfort. It may be necessary for you to make an appointment with the teacher and utilize one of the additional communication strategies aimed at providing immediate resolutions mentioned above.

Homework issues can be challenging. Homework is usually the "practice" or reinforcement part of learning, and through homework you can act as an advocate for your child and the teacher at the same time by

- establishing a structure that works for your family about when and where homework will be completed,
- instilling in your child the importance of giving one's best effort, and

- bringing questions and concerns generated by the home-work back to the classroom so that the teacher can have the opportunity to clarify and keep learning experiences positive.

Getting the Teacher to Make a Change

In the process of addressing concerns about any of your child's school experiences, you may wish to work with the teacher so that something the teacher does or says that affects your child will be changed or modified. The following guidelines can assist you in working toward this as well as to continue to prevent relatively small issues from becoming larger ones.

Separate facts from feelings when listening to your child's version of a situation. Try to adopt a just-the-facts-please attitude at first. It is easy for children to mistake what they wish had happened from what actually has occurred. In fact, you may never find out for sure what really happened, nor is that knowledge always necessary. Don't automatically take your child's version as the only accurate interpretation. Listen carefully for exaggeration and misunderstanding. Ask for details in a caring and nonthreatening manner. You might ask, "What were you doing when the teacher spoke to you?" or "What were the other children doing?" While it's necessary for your child to understand that the situation itself is important, it may be just as crucial for you to comfort your child and provide reassurance rather than get involved with the teacher.

Repeat your child's version of events back to the child, without being judgmental. Review what was just said: "So, this is what happened." This exchange gives children the opportunity to clarify what occurred. It may become obvious that whatever happened wasn't as awful or upsetting as originally thought. Repeating the story will also increase your own understanding if you do decide to become further involved. This father thought he was listening to his son, but he might have investigated more thoroughly before acting.

Nick, a first grader, told his father that he was "beaten up" at recess. Without checking out Nick's story further or looking to see if Nick had any bruises, his father became enraged and immediately went to the principal to complain, threatening to sue the school and implying that what happened was the result of poor supervision. The principal asked Nick to explain his version of the incident while his father was present.

Nick said that the other child was demonstrating his latest karate moves and Nick got flipped. He had not been beaten. The incident had not gone unobserved by the teacher, who had previously told the other child that practicing karate was not allowed. Had Nick's father questioned his son calmly and gotten the facts, he would have been able to better assess the seriousness of the situation. He may still have wanted to speak with the teacher to make sure it wouldn't happen again, but he probably would not have needed to go to the principal.

If you believe a conference with the teacher is necessary, call the school to make an appointment by asking the secretary to have the teacher call you back. This could occur during the teacher's planning time, lunch, at the end of the school day, or in the evening. It is unlikely that the teacher will be called out of class to speak with you. Rather than be in the position of waiting at home for the teacher to call back, it's easier to specify to the secretary when you can be reached. It is also helpful to state your purpose.

When you speak with the teacher, allow for the possibility of misunderstanding or misinterpretation by all involved parties. Try to remain open to the possibility that you or the teacher, or your child could be mistaken—even if you're convinced you know what happened. Saying, "I'm not sure if I understand completely what Brian has told me, but it seems that he feels upset about what happened today while he was giving his report. Can you help clarify things?" will relax the teacher and create a cooperative atmosphere without defensiveness or denial.

Tatiana, a fourth grader, came home upset because she thought the teacher said that the report on astronauts was due in three days. Tatiana's mother thought this was unfair and called the teacher. It was discovered that only the outline was due in three days. Tatiana heard "three days" but missed the main point. It is important to check out what was said to avoid misunderstandings.

Teachers may not be able to recall every detail of an incident. What happened to a child at lunch may have been one of a dozen incidents that day. If you call the teacher to find out what happened, try to clarify rather than interrogate. The teacher may be unable to explain just what occurred. One teacher said, "I'm sorry I wasn't there. I've heard both sides and I'll follow through on it by trying to pay attention to who sits with whom at lunch."

Avoid shouting, insulting, or otherwise threatening the teacher. If something has caused you to be angry, you might say, "I really felt angry when I heard you tore up his paper because you couldn't read his handwriting." But it's wise to avoid sounding hostile or becoming agitated. Be conscious of your voice level. Neither of you will benefit from a shouting match.

Alice Allegro, a fourth-grade teacher, notes, "The parent should appreciate the importance of a polite and respectful relationship with teachers." When a teacher feels pushed or backed against the wall, the outcome may be unsatisfactory. Approach can make all the difference. When you say, "My daughter doesn't want to go out to recess. We think you're letting the kids gang up on her," the teacher may feel threatened. But when you try a softer approach, saying instead, "My daughter doesn't want to go out to recess. Is there anything you have noticed on the playground that can help us understand why she feels this way?" the teacher will be able to better respond and work with you toward a resolution.

If you decide to bring a matter to the principal, the teacher will appreciate knowing that you are taking that step. Even if you have been unable to resolve the issue at your meeting with the teacher, going to the principal without the teacher's knowledge may strain your relationship with the teacher. You can say, "I'm sorry, Mr. Stack, but I feel that we haven't been able to come to agreement on this. I'd appreciate discussing this with our principal." (See Chapter 6.) Families may not realize the message behind their actions. For instance, not telling teachers of your plans can cause them to feel that they are not valued. If left out of the meeting altogether, teachers may feel their point of view will not be shared with the principal, causing mistrust.

If you are angry with the teacher, avoid communicating it through your child.   As previously noted, if you express your disapproval or irritation about a teacher to your child, it places the child squarely—and unfairly—in the middle. Parents unfortunately don't always realize the impact of their comments on their children. Your child may be confused if you say, "How dare Ms. Smith keep you after school—she has some nerve!" Such statements can undermine the respect your child has for the teacher.

You can be honest with your child by thinking carefully before directly expressing negative comments. You may be able to soften your comment and say, "I'm concerned about Ms. Smith keeping you after school. I think I'll write her a note." This indicates your interest but not your outrage and leaves the door open for a positive outcome.

Accept the reality that everyone makes mistakes.   As previously mentioned, it is not easy to approach a teacher and point out a mistake even when you know you're right. A generation ago, most parents believed that teachers just didn't make mistakes. But what if the teacher is giving the children incorrect information?

> In reviewing the process for doing long division, Mr. Grant dictated the steps to be used in the wrong order. While doing homework, you notice your child becoming frustrated and shouting, "This math is stupid. I can't do it. I hate that man!" What do you do?

You don't have to be an expert to know that giving incorrect information such as this can be damaging. If brought to the attention of Mr. Grant, preferably by your child, Mr. Grant can reteach the lesson before incorrect information becomes ingrained. When teachers let their students know that they too make mistakes, real learning takes place.

Give everyone the chance to discuss a change, make the change if appropriate, and then look beyond it.   When you and the teacher genuinely have a trusting relationship, it is easier for everyone to come out a winner. The statement "I know you would want me to ask this" is a measure of such trust. Instead of becoming defensive or feeling threatened, most teachers will welcome your question, think things over, and make a change. There will always be a teacher who can't accept an error or will be unwilling to look at things from your perspective. You then must decide to what extent is it to your child's benefit to keep pushing. Some things may never get fully resolved.

Give teachers credit for their judgment.   You may not realize that an approach being used in the classroom is supported by research. When a parent came in Joan Gibbs's fourth-grade class to complain about the spelling program, the parent didn't realize that it had worked beautifully for the last five years. Although the teacher may need to alter the program to meet her son's individual learning needs, his mother would have been much better off if she had validated the teacher and the program by saying, "I see you are committed to using this program but . . ." rather than, "Can't you see this just isn't helping him spell better?" If you take an opposing stand, it is likely that the person whose mind you are trying to change will only become more entrenched. But when you let that person know that you understand his or her position, you are showing respect and setting the stage for a collaborative rather than an adversarial relationship. Change is more likely to occur in this climate.

Expect progress in small increments rather than giant leaps.   You could even discover that what you believe is the problem may turn out to be just the tip of the iceberg. One parent had concerns about the room in which her son received math help. The room had no windows and was always too warm. Because the child also complained of headaches on the days he used the room, the mother questioned whether it should be used for instruction. After speaking to the teacher and the principal, who had heard similar concerns from other parents, a temporary solution was devised: the placement of a fan in the room. Although the parent had hoped for a different room assignment, this was not possible because of overcrowding in the building. The broader solution would involve looking into the allocation of space within the entire school by the principal and school community.

Explain how you see things.   It's helpful to teachers when families tell them the consequences at home of what is happening in school. Letting teachers know what you hear and see at home gives them clues about what to say or avoid saying to children in school. Sharing your observations and perceptions gives the teacher an opportunity to rethink what is happening in class. Comments such as "Heather worries that by commenting on her new eyeglasses you're suggesting that you don't like them," "Philip says you never ask him to pass out papers," "Gail says she can't learn her math facts because her group is going too fast," or "Jamal is crying himself to sleep at night because he's afraid you'll call on him when he doesn't raise his hand" all help a teacher to know your child better and serve to improve communication among you.

Make sure everyone stays on track.   Try to keep focused on the reason for your meeting. If the teacher wants to use the time you have together to talk about other issues, you might say, "Mr. Smith, I am also concerned about what happened with my daughter's history project, but I'd prefer to talk about whether changing her study group in science will help her get along better with other children. If we could address the social issue first, that will make me feel a lot better." The teacher will recognize and respect your needs.

At the conclusion of the meeting or conversation, make sure you understand what has been said and end with a sense of resolution.   It's a good idea to wrap up by restating your position and what you understand the teacher's position to be: "As I understand it, we've both agreed that Polly's habit of interrupting you is something to work on. You feel that she does it when she's nervous and I feel that she may be doing it because she isn't getting enough feedback from you." Then ask the teacher specifically how the problem will be approached in the future, including what's to be expected from you, the teacher, and the child. Ask how the child's behavior will be evaluated and what the plan is for follow-up: "Should we be back in touch next week or in two weeks?" Don't hesitate to discuss details:

> I want to make sure I'm clear on the plan of action. First, you will try to respond to Polly more often. Second, I will tell Polly she needs to raise her hand quietly, without thrashing around. Third, when you see her hand is up, you'll acknowledge her with your eye to let her know you've seen her. We'll all know she is doing better when the interruptions are less frequent or if they disappear altogether.

If Things Don't Go Your Way

Although the effects of change are often positive, the process of implementing a change may be difficult and can take time. Because of this, you might find that your effort may be less successful than you originally anticipated.

Even if you have followed every suggestion offered, you may be disappointed or feel prevented from achieving your goal. It is frustrating when the teacher listens, acts supportive, and shows slight flexibility but basically doesn't budge. Although teachers say they will be open to you and encourage your input, there are times when you are positive that the teacher doesn't understand or won't meet you halfway.

Since every situation is different, your reactions can vary. You can accept the situation feeling personally put down and out. You can make further attempts to get the teacher to see the situation in a different light, which may require you to provide the teacher with new information. Or you might conclude that in your attempt to implement a change, you actually became supportive of the teacher's view or agreed on something in between that was comfortable for everyone.

It may be helpful to keep three thoughts in mind:

Perceptions vary. As noted earlier, your values and background influence the way you see things. Differing perceptions do not necessarily mean that one view is right and the other is wrong, only that you and the teacher may look at the same situation differently. In addition, being self-righteous could indicate an unwillingness to see the other side. It is important to work together to arrive at an understanding based on mutual satisfaction.

Keep an open mind. When families and schools share their knowledge and perspectives, growth can occur on everyone's part. Knowing when to hold your ground and when to be flexible is difficult, but it always helps to be open-minded and willing to learn.

Follow your gut feelings. After going through suggested procedures, demonstrating sensitivity, and listening well, there may be times when you think you're on the right track and the school is not. At this point, decide whether the issue is worth pursuing. If it is, be persistent and bring your concerns to the principal or other appropriate school personnel. (See Chapters 3 and 6.)

When Something Offends You Deeply

A fifth-grade teacher made a reference to human reproduction during science class. When Clara, a student in the class, told her two older siblings, they listened and added what they knew about the subject. Clara now knew much more than the teacher shared in class. Hearing this information around the house, and assuming it all had been taught in school, Clara's parents were incensed that even the subject had been introduced and decided to take immediate action.

When this family thought that their daughter had received sex education instruction in school, they were offended and felt compelled to act. Situations that affect your core values can challenge your approach to handling situations constructively. By continuing to keep your cool, you might not cause the upsetting event to "unhappen," but you will enable everyone to deal with whatever occurred or did not occur efficiently.

What are school's procedures for resolving such issues? While policies vary, the following guidelines may be helpful:

- Listen to your child if the child was involved.
- If something occurred in a classroom, confirm it with the teacher.
- If it didn't occur in a classroom, you may wish to inform the classroom teacher regardless.
- Go together to the principal.
- Let the principal assist and guide you further or take over for you.
- Expect a resolution, but give it some time.

How Do You Change School Policy?

How a school or a classroom teacher chooses to handle difficult situations is not usually decided haphazardly. Systemwide policies often clearly explain expected procedures. For instance, if a child is found in school with a weapon, school policy often outlines the process for a principal to follow in dealing with it.

If you object to an existing school policy and want to get it changed or you wish to implement a new one, you may first want to state to yourself exactly why you are pursuing this goal, for whom, and if you are prepared for a major time commitment. After reflecting on these considerations, if you feel strongly about pursuing the matter, expect what may be an uphill but potentially rewarding experience. Here are some suggestions if you choose to go ahead:

- Become knowledgeable by gathering background information and facts about what you want to achieve.
- Prepare to educate everyone—from your child's teacher to the school board—in the area in which they may have insufficient information.
- Enlist support from families or other resources (like the PTO) in your school community.

Join community groups that both enrich your knowledge and support your goals.

Be willing to go through a lengthy process and, at times, to feel alone in your endeavor.

Expect unanticipated complications, legal implications, or delays.

Recognize your limitations.

Conclusion

An important issue in handling problems at school is the recognition of sensitivities. When you stop to consider the sensitivity of those involved, your chances of resolving difficulties will be greater. If you do your best to listen well, get the facts, share your perspective, assist in setting goals, and decide on follow-up, you'll be giving your child and the school the message that you respect relationships. Your primary responsibility is the welfare of your child, and your main objective should be to get the issue resolved as efficiently and effectively as possible.

We can all learn with and from each other. When open and honest channels of communication are maintained, problems can be resolved and good things will happen for students, schools, and families.

Notes

1. Haim Ginott, *Teacher and Child,* New York: Macmillan, 1972.

Chapter 6

Bringing Concerns to the Principal

The Personality of the School

Does the following sound familiar?

> As Richard D'Angelo approached his son Ricky's third-grade classroom, he braced himself for what the teacher would say about Ricky's behavior in class.
>
> Although Mr. D'Angelo had spoken with the teacher before, he was still unsure of how to improve Ricky's disruptive behavior. This time Mr. D'Angelo decided to make sure to ask the teacher exactly what Ricky was doing that was causing a problem.
>
> The teacher said, "When Ricky finishes his work he leaves his seat and distracts other children. This causes the noise level to rise and the class becomes difficult to control. As you know, in the past we have set limits for Ricky that have worked. But things just seem to be getting out of hand. I have a few ideas about some other things we could try."
>
> Mr. D'Angelo was becoming tired of hearing about Ricky's disruptive behavior and was losing patience trying new things. He began to wonder whether there was some undetected reason for the misbehavior and decided it was time to bring the issue to the principal.

Before Mr. D'Angelo visits the principal, it would be helpful for him to possess some background information about principals and their roles in schools.

Every school has its own "culture" or "personality," which reflects the attitudes and values of the school community and determines the formal and informal ways things are handled. Although all members of the school community shape the culture of a school, it is the principal who plays a particularly important role in determining the culture. At Madison Elementary School, there is a principal who prefers a quiet atmosphere during the school day, especially during dismissal. At the end of the day students line up in the corridor near their classrooms and leave the building in almost total silence. In contrast, the principal at Parkside Elementary School is comfortable with a bustling school atmosphere. Observing Parkside during dismissal, one sees that although students are clear about what they have to do, there is continuous interaction among students as everyone seems to move in different directions.

Just as these principals have different expectations for dismissal, they will also have varying styles regarding other aspects of the school day, including how they interact with families. Sensitivity to the culture of your child's school will guide you in deciding when and how to bring a concern to the principal.

Do You Remember Your School Principal?

As suggested in Chapter 1, memories from your own childhood can also determine how you respond to issues at your child's school, particularly when bringing your concerns to the principal. Just as you might have been taught not to question the teacher, you might have great reservations about questioning or approaching the principal. Parents in previous generations may have been unlikely to go to a principal with a concern, especially if the principal's style was similar to the following:

Ms. Oster was believed to run the "tightest ship in town." In addition to being a firm disciplinarian, she insisted on maintaining an immaculate school. She was even known for prohibiting children from gathering inside the front entrance of the school on rainy days because it would wear out the carpet. Because of Ms. Oster's stern demeanor, children tended to be fearful of her and parents were reluctant to share their concerns with her.

Whether she realized it or not, Ms. Oster intimidated families by the tone she established in her school. She did not encourage the school community to reach out to her. Ms. Oster's personal style overshadowed the fact that she was highly effective when confronting issues such as homework, school safety, curriculum, or needs of an individual child.

To Go or Not to Go

With a principal whose leadership style resembles that of Ms. Oster, asking for help with a problem might be difficult—although you could be pleasantly surprised once you got into the office. But even when a principal is welcoming, relaxed, and more casual, sharing a concern can be tricky. A combination of the personality of your child, your family's style, the teacher's style, and the culture of your school all work together. What follows are some options available to you when considering whether to bring a concern to the principal.

Ignore the problem or take a wait-and-see approach, hoping that things will clear up on their own. For many families, going to the principal is considered a last resort. One parent said, "Getting involved with the principal is like getting into something legal. I still feel childlike myself. It's hard to shed those feelings even as an adult."

Speak with the teacher. "I was concerned that my son's handwriting had been deteriorating but no one at school had mentioned anything to me. Finally I asked the teacher about it myself. Now that we're both aware of my concern, we can work together to determine how to proceed."

Have your child speak with the teacher. "My daughter's snack was disappearing every day. When I suggested that she speak with the teacher a small problem was resolved and it was prevented from becoming a larger one."

Accept reports from one family to another.   One mother was concerned about why her fourth grader was using blocks in her math class. The mother's friend, whose child was also in the class, had the same concerns. After speaking with the teacher and the principal, the first mother better understood the reasoning for the use of blocks and gave the information to her friend. The explanation was satisfactory. (The principal discovered, however, that other families may also have had a need for more information about the math program.)

Decide if it is the principal who can best help you or whether you should speak with another staff member.   "I was worried that Adam was having trouble jumping rope since I observed that most of his friends could. I went to the physical education teacher. She not only assured me that children learn to do this at different rates, but also offered to show me how to help him practice." (See Chapter 3.)

Go directly to the principal.   "We were quite concerned that sixth grade was too young to have sex education classes in school. The principal supportively said, 'Here is the curriculum we plan to review with parents. Let's talk about your concerns now, and again, after you've had a chance to look it over."

Take a Closer Look at Your Motivation

It's easy to magnify a concern out of proportion. Frustration and anger can cause you to overreact or make demands that the principal might view as unreasonable. If you're about to request something drastic such as having your child placed in a different classroom, realize that these changes happen only rarely and there are many intermediate steps that need to be taken before such a change would be made.

Although principals are ready to hear any problem, it helps to look at the big picture and keep things in perspective. While you may think that the solution to your problem is obvious, the principal may see things differently. It is important to try to be realistic. It is also helpful to principals if you can share definite examples of your concern rather than a feeling that something isn't right.

There is a fine line between being appropriately assertive and inappropriately pushy. You can differentiate this as one principal said, "by keeping focused on the real needs of your child . . . The potential always exists to try to win an adult victory and lose sight of what the real purpose is." The best results for your child will be achieved if your requests reflect this attitude.

Try to answer these initial screening questions before you proceed to the principal:

- What outcome would be best for my child?
- Should I try again to work things out with the teacher before involving the principal?
- Am I prepared for the teacher to learn about this conversation even though I have not informed the teacher about what I am doing?
- Am I acting in the midst of strong emotions?
- Am I beginning to fall into a pattern of habitually bringing concerns to the principal?

If you're still not sure about whether to bring your concern to the principal, consider these questions to help you focus:

- Do I think there is something destructive to the growth of my child occurring?
- Have I tried to work things out with the teacher first and not made progress?
- Is the teacher's plan of action just not working?
- Is this a situation that goes beyond the teacher's expertise?
- Is this a matter of school or district policy?

If the response to any of these questions is still yes, and you have considered the suggestions in the remainder of this chapter, it is reasonable to seek guidance from the principal.

What Kinds of Concerns May Justify Your Going Directly to the Principal?

The following examples of general issues may not focus specifically on your child alone:

- How much involvement should classroom volunteers have in teaching?
- Why is the math program being taught this way? We've had five different programs over seven years!
- Why are test scores so low?
- I'm concerned about safety on the school busses.
- Classes are too crowded.

These issues may focus specifically on your child:

- How do I get extra support for my child?
- The teacher appears to make frequent factual errors in the process of her teaching. I'm concerned that she just doesn't have sufficient command of the material.
- My child is not being challenged in this school.
- I suspect abuse (or other inappropriate behavior).
- The teacher and I disagree on how to teach my child.

Principals also like to hear about things that are going well! A principal's entire day can consist of solving problems. Letting the principal know how pleased you are with the way a problem was resolved or how much you appreciate a change in school policy can make a principal's day. It is not necessary to make an appointment. A note or telephone call is sufficient.

The Way the Principal Sees Things

George Cromwell, a father who worked at home, was the first person Billy saw upon returning from school each day. Invariably Billy's first statement was, "The teacher yelled at me again." At first George didn't think much of it. He knew from previous teachers that Billy didn't follow directions well.

But then Mr. Cromwell remembered a conversation he overheard among a group of parents recently. The gist of it was the teacher doesn't like boys. He wondered whether this was an issue to take to the principal.

This may ultimately be an issue to share with the principal. But first Mr. Cromwell needs to speak with Billy and the teacher about the yelling. If you are confronted with a similar situation, you may wish to consider some aspects of the principal's perspective before deciding what to do.

Part of the principal's job involves guiding families through the process of resolving issues. As at work, where you often learn on the job, you will learn as you go along what's expected of you at school. Your principal will be your best guide.

If you think you have no time to follow a process, you could stumble without even knowing it. Eventually you could begin to feel unsupported or isolated. In situations such as these, you might never be able to get the principal to see things your way.

Once you take an issue to the principal, your future relationship with any teachers involved could change. Many teachers feel threatened when families go to the principal about an issue that they believe directly involves them. Think beforehand about how getting the principal involved will affect your relationship with that teacher. One teacher said, "Do you know what it feels like to have a parent speak to the principal and not say anything to the teacher about it first? It makes the teacher feel left out and interferes with the relationship between the family and the teacher."

The principal's job requires a delicate balance. Have you said to a principal, "I'd appreciate it if you would get the teacher to change, but please don't tell her that I came to see you?" A principal who frequently hears requests to get teachers to change without mentioning the source of the complaint said, "This type of situation paralyzes the principal. We can't be effective if we can't talk to teachers."

It is likely the principal doesn't know the reason for your appointment or even that a problem exists. Essentially you have prepared for this meeting and the principal has not. You may have all the available information about your concern, particularly if it is specific to your child, and the principal may have no information. Expect to help the principal catch up.

> When Ben's mother went to see the principal she incorrectly assumed that he knew all about the parents' misgivings about having a fifth grade dance. Only when the principal said, "Let's back up so I can understand the situation better," was it clear that the principal didn't have a clue as to what the parent was talking about.

Communication lines among all parties involved are often unclear. Who has spoken to whom, who has the facts, how they have they been interpreted, and who is aware of the situation all need to be sorted out by the principal. It may take more time than you expect to learn all aspects of a particular issue.

> Lunchroom procedures were confusing. Several parents complained to the lunchroom supervisor that their children had not received their school lunch. Not until the principal learned of the mix-up would she know how to respond to the parent in her office. She had to investigate first.

There is no guarantee that the principal will immediately comply with your wishes. When you bring a concern to the principal, addressing it often requires more than verbal support. You want the principal to do something. While you ultimately might bring about a change, it is unlikely to happen on demand. Getting extra help for your child, altering a bus route, or even requesting that the bathrooms be better supplied all take time and must go through appropriate channels.

Principals appreciate parents expressing concerns in a non-threatening manner. There are times when an issue is brought to a principal and it involves the parent's word against the teacher's. Suppose you and the teacher have conflicting views and you both have asked the principal to intervene. You said, "Ms. Horgan has been humiliating Nancy in front of the class," while Ms. Horgan disagrees. This kind of confrontation is difficult to resolve, yet a skilled principal will handle this so that no one feels put down in public. You can help by saying instead, "Nancy comes home upset when you have called her name out loudly in class. She says this embarrasses her in front of her classmates." While the teacher's behavior is still called into question, the concern also expresses the consequences for Nancy and allows the principal to support both sides in resolving the difficulty.

Arranging Your Meeting

Once you've decided to meet with the principal, it's important to recognize that she or he has a busy schedule. Just as you wouldn't expect a doctor to see you without an appointment unless it is urgent, it's unrealistic to assume that the principal will be able to meet with you immediately. You might consider the following:

- Make an appointment through the school secretary.
- If you think it is an emergency, say so. You might be asked to reveal the reason for your visit.
- By giving a short summary of the reason for your visit to the secretary even if it is not an emergency, you enable the principal to prepare for your meeting and avoid the need to catch up.
- Let the secretary know your work schedule or time limitations and ask whether a telephone meeting might be sufficient if it is difficult for you to come in person.
- If you are not sure whether your concern can wait, ask the secretary to run it by the principal. Ask that you get a call back as to how to schedule the appointment.
- If the principal encourages families to drop in do so.

However, don't ask the principal, "Do you have a minute?" and then stay for thirty!

- Try to think about whatever time you must wait for the appointment as a cooling off period. This will help you collect your thoughts.

The Principal's Principles: Guiding Families Through Process

Principals have found that most problems can be handled success-fully by the classroom teacher. After listening to your concern, the principal may ask, "Have you talked to Mr. Austin, Glenn's teacher about this?" If you answer yes, you are on relatively safe ground. Remember that although you may have discussed the issue with the teacher, he or she may be unaware of your meeting with the principal. Some principals consider this going over the teacher's head. Others feel comfortable with it.

What the principal might prefer you to reply is, "I have spo-ken to Mr. Austin about Glenn's reading and he knows that we are meeting today." This response enables the principal to speak with you knowing that you and the teacher have been open with each other. This should result in a meeting that is productive.

Once you've approached most principals, unless it is already obvious that the teacher has not been involved, any of the follow-ing could happen:

If you're reluctant to speak with the teacher, the principal may help you participate in resolving the issue.

Sue Cosby, Andrea's mother, was concerned that Andrea's reputation as teacher's pet was becoming a problem. At first it seemed cute that the teacher, Ms. Williams, gave her lots of attention. The teacher complimented her on her good work and always seemed to give her opportunities to accept positions of responsibility in the class. Other students must not have minded this and maintained respect for Andrea because she had emerged as a leader in the class.

But lately things have changed. Andrea has started to call her mother at work to complain about the kids calling her teacher's pet. Andrea didn't seem to have as many friends asking her to play after school as she once did and, most important, she was starting to lose her self-confidence. Ms. Cosby made an appointment with the principal.

Ms. Cosby didn't feel right about going to the teacher so she asked the principal to take over. The principal, however, was not comfortable with this approach. Solving the problem meant helping Ms. Cosby become confident at bringing the concern to the teacher herself. This was accomplished by:

- Finding out from the parent what prevented her from speaking to the teacher. What is the worst thing that could happen?
- Role-playing or practicing a conversation between the parent and the teacher.
- Offering to be present and/or facilitate a discussion between the two parties.

If you are reluctant to speak with the teacher, the principal may be willing to handle your concern without requiring you to communicate with the teacher. Some principals are comfortable having families bring concerns to them without insisting that they speak to the teacher first. Principals may view this as an opportunity for families to bring their issues to a neutral party. If this is the practice in your child's school, comply with it but do so knowing that it is acceptable to share your thoughts with the classroom teacher as well. In such settings, teachers may expect the principal to resolve conflicts in this way and are comfortable with this process.

The principal will request that you go back to the teacher and discuss the issue with the teacher first. It is generally in the best interest of your relationship with the teacher and best for your child if you communicate openly with the teacher first.

Whether or not you think the teacher is doing a good job, the teacher connects you and your child with the educational system. The principal can be most helpful to you knowing you have a trusting, working relationship with the teacher. (See Chapter 4.)

Ms. Cosby attempted to go over the teacher's head. The problem could have become worse if the principal hadn't encouraged her to go back to the teacher first. The teacher, believing that she should have been given an opportunity to speak with the parent first, would no longer trust Ms. Cosby as she previously had.

Let's assume that you have spoken to the teacher and you sense that progress is slow. If the teacher does not suggest getting an opinion from the principal, you can do this by saying to the teacher, "Ms. Johnson, I know we've talked about the kids picking on John. We gave it some time and tried the things you suggested but John is still upset. Would you mind if we asked our principal if he could help?"

Even if the teacher does not like this idea, you have been forthright and shown respect for the teacher. If the teacher agrees, set up an appointment with all three of you. If the teacher does not agree, set one up for the principal and you knowing that you have done your best to ensure a positive relationship with the teacher. The principal will be free to act on everyone's behalf.

The principal will tell the teacher about your conversation. If it is not your principal's style to insist that you speak to the teacher, the principal may still have a need to share your conversation with the teacher. Principals will often let you know that they plan to do this, but you might ask.

If, however, you have not told the teacher you were going to speak with the principal, the teacher may be surprised to hear about it from the principal. The teacher's thinking might be, "Obviously, Ms. Cosby is upset. If I had been given an opportunity to discuss things with Ms. Cosby and Andrea, something could have been pointed out to me that I didn't realize I was doing. But I never had a chance. How can I continue to trust her?"

The principal will arrange an appointment with all three of you. This arrangement eliminates guessing about what was said. It maximizes openness and encourages communication. One principal said, "I do this a lot—it keeps the mystery out of the discussion, forms a team to solve problems, and eliminates the 'he said/she said' aspect."

The only difficulty you might find is in your confidence in participating at a meeting with two staff members. Even if it is your first time you can participate in a meaningful way. When everyone can sift things out, you can all look at the facts, evaluate the alternatives, and decide together on how to proceed.

As You Sit in the Principal's Office

Think of yourself as a link between your child and the school. By providing the school with valuable insights about your child, you are making it possible for you and the principal to work together for your child's benefit. What follows are some suggestions that will help you make the meeting productive.

- Be yourself. Speak clearly and plainly. Have your facts correct.
- In stating your concerns, ideas, and suggestions, focus on the issues and on what would be best for your child. It may be helpful to prepare your thoughts in writing.
- Explain what approaches you think have already been undertaken to resolve the problem.
- Be prepared to be asked questions or have an idea presented you had not considered. This may cause you to think about things differently.
- Take notes.
- Expect that the principal will use as little educational jargon as possible, but if you do not understand something, ask for clarification.
- Be patient. Change does not occur overnight.
- Be prepared to accept an outcome that may be different from the one you expected or hoped for. Compromise may be necessary.
- Even if you are an educator or are aware of the latest research relevant to your concern, avoid projecting an

attitude that suggests you are telling staff members how to do their jobs.

- Expect criteria for goal achievement to be set. You might ask, "How are we going to know whether Adina is being challenged? How will her behavior tell us?"

- Make sure the meeting ends with a discussion of a time-table for solving the problem.

- Express appreciation and, if you think it would be help-ful, ask the principal for a written summary of what was decided.

Seeing Eye to Eye with the Principal

Leadership styles vary. When the style of the principal is consistent with your needs, it is relatively easy to establish a positive work-ing relationship. If the principal's style and expectations are differ-ent from what you envision, you might find it more difficult to communicate effectively. Principals can be effective leaders and communicate with families successfully regardless of their style. Try not to be discouraged from approaching your principal because your styles are different.

It is possible, however, that a principal may not support your view or agree with you. You may choose to accept this. If not, the following suggestions are ways to encourage the principal to look at the issue in a different light.

Provide the principal with new information. You may be certain that your son John's immature behavior should not prevent him from being promoted to second grade. By sharing with the school your observations of John's behavior in situations that the school may not be able to see or by providing an assessment from a resource the school is not aware of, the principal or others in-volved may be willing to rethink the original proposal.

Ask the principal to help you get more information. There are times when you are not sure what is right yourself but you want the principal to rethink a decision with you by exploring a situation further. You may want to suggest some ideas: "Let's see how she does during the summer," or, "May we test her again just to be sure she was not having a bad day?" Understand, though, that most decisions are based on more than one test, observation, or event. It is patterns of behavior or several factors that are weighed in making decisions. Even with new information, the original thinking may remain unchanged. But by adding new data—whether you're concerned about a particular school policy affecting many or want to make the best decision for your child—the principal's perceptions may be changed.

What if you reach an impasse?   If after carefully assessing the situation you believe that the response of the principal is not acceptable to you, explain this to the principal and discuss it. If you think that you must share your concern with a different administrator, be open and honest about letting the principal know. This will give the principal an opportunity to continue to be involved. Even if you don't agree, you will be respected.

Ways Families Can Help the Principal

An experienced principal offers the following additional suggestions for families to consider when meeting with a principal:

- Represent yourself (not others from the soccer field or the neighborhood). When a parent calls or comes reporting that "Many, many people think. . . ." it is difficult to operate on this theory. Unless "many, many" people come to see the principal, it is still assumed to be one person's issue.
- Don't save it up. July 1, after the school year is over, is not a good time to come and list the year's problems. There is little that can be done at that time.
- Share positive thoughts as well as negative.
- Some families are reluctant to speak to the principal due to a concern that doing so will be held against their child. This is not the case. If anything, the school staff will be more careful in their words and actions. Educators take their professional responsibilities very seriously

and will not benefit by jeopardizing their relationships with school families in this way.

- As long as you present thoughts in a positive, respectful manner and are open to other points of view, the school can continue to grow and flourish as a result of your feedback.

Conclusion

Think about how important a meeting with the principal is to you and to the well-being of your child and then decide whether to proceed. It is worthwhile to express concerns, but taking them to the principal before speaking to the teacher(s) involved can present problems.

Your goal, as in all dealings with the school, should be that of working with rather than working against. This attitude will help you achieve what is best for your child. Remember that the same situation can look very differently from the principal's, the teacher's, your child's, and your own perspective.

Principals want to keep the communication between parents and teachers open because this approach is healthy for your child and allows everyone to maintain mutual respect.

The following is an excerpt from a message another principal would offer to families:

> Share what you know about your children with us. Tell us about their strengths, their fears, and their joys. Tell us what we do that helps them thrive and what we do that doesn't. Tell us what you need to know more about in order to support their learning. Work with us to open up that wondrous world of learning to your children.

Chapter 7

Volunteering: A Worthwhile Opportunity to Serve Your School Community

Another Committee?

Perhaps the family in the following scenario resembles your own.

Everyone is awake early. Lunches are made, the children are sent to the bus stop, and you're off to work yourself. In the afternoon your children go to after school activities and you have a meeting that lasts into the dinner hour. To your chagrin, you arrive home to find the children watching television and eating junk food to fight off their hunger. Tired, you magically create a dinner at which everyone recalls something that happened to them that day. You make a few telephone calls, try to give each child some "quality time," and if you're lucky, by nine-thirty the house starts to settle down. You glance at a notice from school asking you to chaperone your daughter's class to the local zoo. Not loving zoos, you remember doing something like this once before and coming home exhausted. Besides, what do they expect you to do, take time off from work? "No way. You'll have to find somebody else!" you mumble.

It is easy to let this request slide by. Given the stress caused by hectic schedules in many families, it is not surprising that volunteering often carries a low priority. One frustrated parent asked, "Don't they know that families are busy, with almost no time to help out at school?"

Yet despite the forces preventing families from getting involved expanding school populations, shrinking budgets, and maintaining a home-school connection cause schools to reach out to families more than ever. Recognizing this conflict, schools are challenged to simultaneously juggle sensitivity to your needs at home while encouraging you to become involved in school life.

In the past mothers were the expected volunteers. Today it is not uncommon for fathers, grandparents, older siblings, live-in baby-sitters, or even an aunt or uncle to participate in school life. A grandparent who was initially uncomfortable with any involvement at school said, "At first whenever I entered my granddaughter's school I felt a bit foolish as if the school were not my territory, but I now see things differently."

In addition, many communities encourage senior citizens to volunteer in schools. They may do this by assisting teachers in classrooms, sharing special skills, or participating in intergenerational programs.

The Role of the PTO

Many volunteer activities are coordinated through the parent-teacher organization in your school. Often known as the PTA, this vital resource is available to all families in the school community and functions as a vehicle for communication between home and school. With increased emphasis on family involvement in children's education, PTOs reach out to parents and teachers.

Although PTOs function differently and some are more active than others, their goals are often achieved through fund-raising, educating families about changes in education, or providing support for families in the school community. Through guest speakers, breakfasts, or newsletters, PTOs provide opportunities for parents to share their views as well as reflect on their roles as parents. As one former PTA president said, "The PTA provides an opportunity for the linking of education and the realities of life."

PTOs may also collaborate with school staff to study issues directly related to your child's school experience. Committees explore issues such as school safety, use of school space, or technology in the schools. The PTO is a unique forum for facilitating positive change in the school community.

Is Volunteering a Chore or a Pleasure?

Volunteering can enhance your relationship with the school as well as provide an opportunity to support it. But whether organized through the PTO or under the direction of others, volunteering is not for everyone. Time constraints are not the only deterrent. You might have had unpleasant experiences because no one directed you or appreciated your efforts. If your needs were not met, volunteering could easily have been viewed as a chore rather than a pleasure. Is it possible that unclear expectations or breakdowns in communication interfered with your experience as a volunteer?

Some of the issues below may still be keeping you away. Perhaps as you read about them you will begin to look at the process of volunteering in a different light.

"I'm always asked to do the same thing."   Volunteer acts run the gamut—assisting with a reading group, helping edit the school newspaper, shelving books in the library one hour a week, and working on school traffic issues. The range of volunteer activities is extensive.

Varying levels of responsibility and decision making are inherent in volunteer tasks. Some require you to utilize your organizational skills such as coordinating volunteer programs, planning fund-raising events, or running an international night at school. Others require your continuing participation in ongoing school programs such as handicapped awareness or membership on a community-wide committee to study curriculum. Some activities involve working closely with children. Others do not. Some require your presence in school. Others you can do at home. Although you may have been channeled into a particular role there may be others that better meet your needs.

"I did more when the children were younger, and besides, my child doesn't want me there."   As children get older, their interest in having family members in the classroom or school changes, sometimes causing them to become embarrassed and uncomfortable when their parents are involved at school. As a result, your level of involvement may change.

> Linda's mother was self-employed. When the children were small she arranged her schedule so she could work on Tuesday evenings when her husband was home to care for the children, which freed her to help in the school library every Tuesday morning. Linda loved it when her mother came to school each week during her library period. But as Linda has gone into sixth and seventh grade, having her mother in school doesn't seem to be as important to her as it used to be.

But must families stay away completely? One fifth grader pleaded with his mother, "Please stay out of my classroom." When questioned he said, "None of my friend's parents ever help in the class." Staying away from your child's classroom may be best in this case. If you become involved in an activity like working in the library when your child is not present, you can respect your child's preferences and still provide an important service to the school. While your own child's interest may wane, the school still appreciates whatever assistance you can provide.

"I'm afraid of making a fool of myself."   It is not easy to enter a classroom, even when you have something special to share. One parent who had been invited to speak to a group of youngsters about his profession found that he was intimidated by the classroom. An atmosphere dominated by the authority of the teacher, uncertainty of how to handle a disruption, concern about speaking at a level the students would understand, and thoughts of failing in front of his own child created a stressful situation. By letting the teacher know about his apprehension ahead of time, the teacher could have worked with this parent to prepare for the experience.

"When I do volunteer for a task, I feel as if I'm doing all the work."   In many organizations, whether it is the Little League, the school, or the museum board of trustees, the same people tend to get involved and stay involved. How often have you heard, "The same people do all the work?" "Wouldn't it be nice to see some new faces?"

Do you find that performing your job well only earns you the reputation of being a terrific worker—and your reward is to be given more work? Some people worry that once they say yes they'll be volunteered for everything. One way to approach this is to accept a task as a partnership with a co-worker, perhaps someone who is inexperienced. The experienced person may then teach the job to the new person with the expectation that that person will eventually take over.

"I'm worried that I'm not as competent as everyone else."
It's easy to be scared off by those who act as if they know everything. But everyone has a stake in the school and has something to contribute. If you are willing to take a small risk, you might discover exciting rewards. By thinking about specific things you can do that are right for you, these issues may not arise. For instance, if you would rather not interact with large groups in a formal way, you may choose to collate a newsletter or take notes at a meeting.

"I know that once I become involved, everything will snowball. I will be urged to attend events I can't. Besides, I'm terrible at saying no." It's no fun to make an excuse, especially if you are a personal friend of the person you're refusing. On the other hand, no one wants to get in over their head. Rest assured that saying yes will not obligate you to continued major commitments. Whatever you do, even making a few telephone calls should be appreciated. Chairpeople can become so involved in their tasks that they expect everyone to share their excitement. While this enthusiasm can motivate some people to give the task their best effort, it can also turn others off. When all one father wanted to do was hang a few decorations for the dance, he found himself on the defensive when asked to chaperone later on. Not feeling appreciated for what he did do, George viewed the added request as an imposition. His perception was, "The more I do, the more they want me to do."

Picture this early morning scene.

At a morning school function, one parent said to another, "Hi, Jan. What are you doing here? I thought you worked mornings."

"I do," said Jan. "They twisted my arm and I just couldn't say no."

Jan should have been able to decline gracefully. Because she was uncomfortable doing this, she juggled her work schedule to go. Unfortunately, resentment often builds up instead of pleasure. If she had replied, "I'd love to come but it's a work day for me," she would have said no and still given the message that she supported the function. Everyone would have understood.

"I'm intimidated by the people involved. They're not my friends and they all seem to know each other. They've formed their own cliques." The unknown can be intimidating and it can be difficult to find your niche in the school community. While those who volunteer may appear to stay with their own friends, everyone works together for the benefit of the school. It is likely that these volunteers probably began their involvement by doing just one thing that felt right for them. You can do the same. Gradually your contacts will increase.

"It is the responsibility of the school to educate the child and the school should not be looking to me for help." This is a complex issue. It raises the question, "Who is supposed to be doing the educating?" Getting the best for your child does not require you to become involved in a prescribed way. Although not everyone can or should be the coordinator of a major school program, adopting a totally hands-off approach at school could give your child and the school the message that you don't care. Even if you can't be involved, it is important to be aware of what is happening at school and to communicate to your child that you are interested.

How you do this depends on your style. It may mean writing a note to the teacher directly on your child's homework paper: "We're delighted that Steven is able to write complete sentences." While different from volunteering, this personal and private communication gives the school and your child the message that you value the teacher's effort.

136

Teachers also realize that family schedules often prevent involvement in classroom activities or in other school events. In communicating this understanding one teacher told a child, "I know how much your family would like to come to the science presentation tomorrow. We'll send a picture and a tape home so they can see what a good job you've done."

In addition to the fundamental support you provide your child at home, giving your time to the school community creates opportunities for students that might not otherwise exist. Whether you help to set up an authors' night, run a booth at the school fair, or read a story to a class, someone benefits from your support.

Jumping In Carefully

If you think you would like to volunteer, consider your motivation before you make a choice. If you identify with any of these factors it may be worthwhile to rethink your decision.

Find Out Where Your Child Stands First

Thinking her son would be pleased, this parent was surprised at his reaction.

> Diane Green was asked to take over the school newspaper, which was published once a month. This would mean a significant time commitment and require her to be in and out of the school on almost a daily basis. She considered her decision and its impact on things at home.
>
> After deciding to take the challenge, she excitedly said to her son, "Guess what, James? I'm going to be spending quite a bit of time at your school working on the newspaper. Isn't that terrific?"
>
> James sighed, "Right, mom. I guess so. Does that mean all my friends and I are going to see you around the school all the time?"

While some children don't care what their families do or don't do in the school or classroom, others have definite opinions. If James and his mother had discussed things before the decision was made, James would have felt included and the decision would have been made with keeping his sensitivities in mind.

Children like James need their own school lives. Being away from family members during the school day encourages their independence and development. One parent also learned from experience. She concluded after many years of volunteering that families can volunteer too much, possibly so that a child's growth can be stifled. By negotiating the needs of both parent and child, children can be listened to and respected.

Consider Whether Your Real Purpose Is to Observe Your Own Child

Everyone likes to see how their child is doing first hand. When your attitudes, assumptions, and expectations about what is happening in school are positive, you can enjoy helping in the classroom and at the same time observe your child interact with the teacher and classmates. But if you have particular concerns about a teacher or your child, using a volunteer opportunity to focus solely on them should be avoided. If nothing else, it detracts from your effectiveness as a volunteer.

Instead, confront your real concerns head on. For instance, if you are worried that your daughter has become withdrawn in the classroom, explain this to the teacher. You might ask, "Do you mind if I come in and watch for a short while?" This is preferable to using your role as a classroom helper strictly to observe.

Think About Whether You Have Any Other Hidden Agenda
Consider the following situation:

> Ms. Walker spent part of almost every day at school either working on the student handbook or on some other worthwhile school project . She could be seen in or about the school office or classrooms, including those of her own children, at any given time. Ms. Walker was so involved that one could not help but think, "She's amazing. Volunteering at school must be the most important thing in her life."

Although there are many dedicated Ms. Walkers who volunteer in schools and genuinely want to help, this Ms. Walker was volunteering because she didn't trust the school. Possibly without even realizing it she had a need to be present as much as possible to satisfy herself that the school was meeting her expectations.

Some have also used their role as a volunteer to try to influence the teacher or principal in some way. One parent assumed that because she was a volunteer and known at school it would be possible to sway a decision about which teacher her child would be assigned the next year. While some schools might go along with this practice, others would view it as a problem and would be unwilling to support it. When you volunteer your time, it is best to do so as a team player rather than as a critic or a participant with other objectives.

"I'm ready to volunteer, but how do I begin?"

Once you've thought through your concerns and considered your basic motivation, just how you decide what job you will undertake varies with your individual style and the needs of the school. There is no right way to determine this. Some volunteers find excitement in plunging into any area that is new and challenging. Others might say, "Just tell me where to report and what you'd like me to do."

You may have a need to use a more focused method of finding the best volunteer niche for you. If so, here are some ways to approach looking at your own strengths:

What expertise do you have to share?   If you have a skill that can be shared with either large or small groups of children, you can be a valuable resource to the school. For instance, if your child's teacher is planning a project where children write their own books, your skill in bookbinding could guide children to assemble their books. Or if the PTO is considering organizing the designing and construction of a new school playground, your experience as a carpenter could be helpful in providing the planning committee with useful information.

How do you feel about being in charge?   Perhaps a leadership role is for you. Taking charge of a task requires setting goals, identifying a plan to achieve them, implementing the plan successfully, and keeping everybody involved and feeling appreciated. This is a challenge that can be extremely rewarding.

What kinds of projects motivate you? Volunteer tasks can be carried out in the larger community, or within the school or individual classroom. As you become aware of choices, identify one that especially interests you. Your enthusiasm will be infectious and you will be seen as an asset in getting the job done. Whether this involves assisting the classroom teacher once a week, organizing the T-shirt sale, or sitting on the school council, enthusiastic volunteers add to the success of the task.

Three Keys to Success

Be reliable. Any volunteer project you undertake should be taken seriously and you must be able to be counted on—even if you're standing behind the coffee urn at the election day bake sale. If you can't get to your post try to inform someone who will be present or is in charge. Otherwise, the job may be delayed, postponed, or never get done. As a volunteer, it doesn't matter if you're filing in the office or going on a field trip: if you're late the impact is felt.

> A schoolwide program was implemented to ensure children's safety by asking families to confirm all absences. Each morning a parent volunteer contacted any family whose child was marked absent without a phone call from home. Failure to call the school could reveal that a child was hurt on the way to school or didn't arrive for an unknown reason, necessitating further investigation.
>
> On a given day, if the scheduled parent volunteer did not appear, this often time-consuming but important job was left to the office staff, who had to add this task to their already busy day.

Just as you would arrive at work on time, reliability is important when you volunteer at your child's school.

Be flexible. If you are asked to help with an activity, but arrive to find you've been switched to a different assignment, how flexible can you be? You may have experienced the following:

> A class trip needed one parent on each of three buses to chaperone a trip to an amusement park for the day. Originally planning to ride on your daughter's bus, the teacher in charge asked you to shift to a different bus. You were disappointed. While it would have been your choice to ride on your daughter's bus, you decided that your job of chaperoning where you were needed was the important issue, not the particular bus you were on.

When explaining your intended plans to your child ahead of time, it is helpful to mention that last minute changes could prevent you from participating exactly as you had thought.

Have a sense of humor. You don't need to be a comedian to be successful as a volunteer. But a little humor goes a long way. Parents, teachers, and children derive unexpected pleasure from each other when everyone can appreciate the lighter side of an issue.

If you plan to spend time with children, expect that as you work to bring out the best in them, they'll bring out the best in you if you keep your sense of humor!

Being Professional in the Classroom

Teachers have different philosophies about inviting volunteers to assist them in their classrooms. They might choose to reach out for any help available, focus only on specific areas where they desire assistance, send out volunteer questionnaires to families to determine assistance, or prefer not to have help.

While volunteer assistance is generally appreciated by teachers, it isn't always as helpful as expected. In fact, it can even create some problems. If volunteers tell the teacher how and what to teach, are frequently late, or lack patience, they might be placing the teacher in a trap between needing help on one hand and accepting uncomfortable arrangements on the other.

Teachers recognize the need to respect differing styles but not to the point of compromising classroom standards. Being a quality volunteer in the classroom essentially requires respecting the teacher's role and being a classroom resource. The following suggestions will help you volunteer with professionalism:

Consider your interest in being with children It is important to be comfortable working with children and genuinely like children when you volunteer in a classroom. Children will be most responsive when your sincerity and patience are evident.

Find out exactly what the teacher wants you to do. Ask the teacher to explain specific expectations in advance or you might find yourself winging it or guessing what to do. If the teacher asks you, "Could you please review number facts with this group of children?" you might want to ask, "How is it best to do this?" Teachers should welcome this opportunity to assist you.

Make an effort to arrive a few minutes early. Just as teachers try to arrive in class early to be ready for children, volunteers may need to speak with a teacher before an activity or class begins. Rather than arrive at the last minute, it is best when you are relaxed and prepared for the children as well.

Be aware of your positioning in the classroom. If you remain in the background—preferably away from the focus of activity—until the teacher is ready for you to participate, you will prevent children from becoming distracted. The teacher will appreciate this and be able to maintain normal classroom practices and routines.

Don't be put off if the teacher does not implement your ideas. With distractions and many needs to meet, teachers can't always give adequate explanations to volunteers. If your suggestion is not implemented or the teacher doesn't seem to support your idea, this should not be taken personally or cause you to question your value to the classroom. On the other hand, if you have a more efficient way of doing something that can be easily carried out and it is impractical to discuss it with the teacher ahead of time, most teachers will appreciate your taking the lead.

Practice some additional basics of classroom volunteering.

- Give attention to all children rather than just your own.
- Avoid unnecessary dialogue with other adults in the classroom.
- If a teacher asks you to do something that makes you uncomfortable, point out something you are comfortable doing instead.
- Your time should be devoted to helping the teacher rather than discussing your own child.
- Understand that your role is to be a support to the teacher.

Leave promptly once the activity is over, respecting the teacher's need to move on to the next part of the day. Even if the teacher stops to chat with you, it's a good idea to take the initiative and say something like, "I know you need to get back to the children. I really enjoyed being here. Thanks for inviting me to help."

The Benefits of Volunteering: What's in It for You?

Volunteering either through the PTO or other vehicles provides organized opportunities for you to directly or indirectly help children. But the outcomes are positive not only for the school and your child; they are positive for you. Some specific areas in which the entire experience becomes worthwhile include:

Personal Growth

Through volunteering you contribute your time and expertise to the school, become known to the school community, and increase your awareness of schoolwide issues. Your own growth can occur inadvertently:

> Skeptical of what the drug education program was all about, Nicole's mother caught the end of a program as she was leaving the building after helping in the library. Just hearing the closing remarks convinced her of the value of

the program and its benefit to students. She not only was more aware of what the program was like, she would now support it.

Relationships are mutually beneficial. You and the school both give to each other. As the school community becomes familiar with you, you will earn a reputation that reflects your involvement and your effort. Your accomplishments in one area can open doors to challenging and stimulating opportunities in others. The rapport that you develop with staff and other families can prove to be an asset and motivate you toward future involvement should you desire it.

Familiarity
The class that you've heard is poorly managed or out of control may not appear as such when you help out in the classroom. Through your involvement you may discover that what you think occurs at school and what may actually occur are quite different. Having an opportunity to view things from inside can increase your understanding of goals, values, and priorities that your school community shares. Your perceptions may change as you experience the culture of the school.

All Children, Including Yours, Will Benefit
Most children (after resolving any concerns about your coming, as discussed earlier) will be pleased to know that a member of their family is helping out at school. Watching you at school gives children an opportunity to observe you in a role different from the one they see at home.

A bond is created when your presence is noticed and acknowledged by other children as well. Word travels fast when there is a familiar adult in the school.

> Harry's father was walking down the second-grade corridor on his way to his son's classroom. The purpose of his visit was to speak about his job at the radio station to the class. But what occurred in the corridor seemed even more important to Harry's dad. Two classes were lining up for their next activity. Like an echo, each child in line who

144

knew him called out, "Hi Mr. Larson" in a warm, friendly gesture that he will always remember.

A Sense of Satisfaction

It is rewarding to be helpful at school. Whether your own children are in the school, in the class, or no longer part of your school environment, you'll feel that you have contributed to the complex workings of an educational system. The act of giving to the community in a way that is timely and right for you is a source of lasting pleasure and satisfaction.

One parent who is a classroom, school, and community volunteer reflected on many years of continuing commitment to the schools by saying, "The teachers do so much for our children that volunteering is my way of saying thank you. The most helpful approach a volunteer can offer says, What can I do? I am available to you.' This allows the teacher to invite the volunteer to participate as a partner and everybody benefits."

When Time Remains an Obstacle

The schools provide a broad spectrum of volunteer possibilities. Here are some suggestions you may wish to try that can be short term and not involve an extended commitment. Many of these activities may be organized by your PTO.

- Help out on a weekend morning for a project such as school beautification.
- Chaperone a single field trip.
- Be available to make telephone calls for the school. Let the person in charge know how many calls you have . time to make.
- Fill orders for a school fund-raiser such as for candy, wrapping paper, or calendars.
- Contribute used books to the classroom library.
- Help provide refreshments for an event.
- Give an hour to run a booth at a school event.
- Assist in the computer lab.

How to Get More Information Before Making a Commitment

You've been home from work for about an hour. The children have dispersed to do their homework. You are still in the kitchen winding down from the day. The telephone rings.

"Hello Jim, this is Frank Mullen, Joey's Dad."
"How are you Frank? How's your family?"
"Everyone's good, thanks. Have you got a minute?"
Jim thinks, "I'll bet he wants me to do something."
"Sure," says Jim. "What can I do for you?"
"Do you remember the Sports Night the school ran with the PTA two years ago? Well, at the meeting the other night, it was brought up as something we ought to do again. Some names were mentioned as possibilities to chair it and yours came up. We all remembered the great job you did organizing our Walk for Hunger last year. What do you say? Will you do it?"

Jim's first instinct might have been to say, "Thanks, but no thanks." However, a few questions came to mind as he was speaking to Frank. The responses Jim received helped him clarify the task. This made it easier for him to make a decision about whether to accept the job.

Here are some questions you can ask if you find yourself in Jim's position.

- What does this job involve?
- How much time at meetings will be necessary?
- Is there a committee already in place or will I be expected to form my own?
- Are there notes or records than can be used from the last time this was done to save time?
- Is there someone available to assist me? If not, may I appoint someone?
- Is it possible to split the job due to time constraints? May a couple of us work together as cochairs and share responsibility equally?

- What difficulties did you encounter last time this was done?
- Do you anticipate any additional difficulties this time?

Note that the person to whom you are speaking might not have all the answers but should be willing to get back to you. In addition, take your time about agreeing. Feeling pressured to answer with a quick yes can result in a decision you could regret. If necessary ask for time to think things over. You might say, "I'd like to mull this over for a while. When would you want me to get back to you?"

Conclusion

The school community reaches out for the support of volunteers who are indispensable resources for schools. While volunteer involvement often takes place within your child's school, a broad spectrum of opportunities exist within the greater community as well. Groups such as school foundations and school councils welcome motivated participants who seek ongoing involvement.

Participate as a volunteer in a way that makes you comfortable. Try not to be concerned about all the things you are not doing or be overwhelmed by volunteer sign-up sheets soliciting your assistance. It takes time to become accustomed to letting others know just what works for your schedule and what doesn't. If the timing isn't right this year, perhaps your needs and interests will change in the future. Whether you take on a leadership role or prefer to keep your involvement limited, each opportunity should provide you with an experience that will involve you in communicating with the school, increase your understanding of how your school works, and provide you with an opportunity to give something to children. As one veteran volunteer says,

> Volunteering gives parents and other significant adults an opportunity to make a difference in children's lives outside the home. Giving of yourself to the school and the community lets children know that you care and are willing to take the time to be there, to help, to impart a particular skill or knowledge, or to basically share of yourself.

Most children are happy and proud to have their family involved either during school hours or at other times. As a volunteer, I was always amazed at how much I could share and help the children, and also how much I learned from them.

Reflections

Having the right tools makes any job easier. By empowering yourself with tools such as effective communication skills, you will relate well to your child's teacher and help your child have a positive school experience. As these approaches gradually become automatic, you may find yourself thinking, "At one time I might have made the situation worse. But now the teacher and I work together rather than in opposition to one another. Things actually do get resolved."

It's best if you are able to address issues without being confrontational. By using a collaborative approach to communication, you will promote an open, honest exchange between you and the teacher. Two parents whose children are now grown were asked what advice they could offer those with younger children. One said, "Never be embarrassed to advocate for your child," and the other noted, "How you approach the teacher is everything." These comments suggest the importance of reaching out on behalf of your child but doing it in a thoughtful manner. Even if things don't work out to your satisfaction or if you feel stuck in a difficult situation, you will leave the door open for further dialogue so that at the very least you can agree to disagree.

Having a clear understanding of the teacher's position as well as your own and letting the teacher know that you appreciate that there are other perspectives will communicate to the teacher that you acknowledge differences of opinion. Saying to a teacher, "I can see why you did this but I still don't think it is right for my child," rather than, "You've handled this all wrong," shows respect for the teacher despite your need to have things addressed differently. This recognition demonstrates that you are a team player, stimulates two-way communication between you and the teacher, and increases the likelihood that the teacher will be open and responsive to your views.

Try to consider the example you are setting for your children by the manner in which you communicate with their teachers. As children become more active participants in communicating their needs at school and at home, they watch, listen, learn, and practice on their own what they see and hear from their families. The best way you can teach your children to be effective communicators is to model these skills yourself.

Communication with school and the teacher can be thought of as a series of messages or signals that you transmit to one another. Something as simple as getting to hear your child's school concert transmits the message that you care. Such messages form patterns and those patterns of behavior and the messages that they communicate express everyone's needs and expectations.

You may have established a pattern of not connecting with the teacher or with the school. There are undoubtedly times when the most appropriate response for you is not to respond at all. But if you consistently choose this route or, conversely, if you react to every issue that comes up, you may be communicating unintentional messages that in the long run may not be in your child's best interest. To avoid being misunderstood, if you make an effort to communicate to the teacher that you support your child and you care, mutual trust and positive feelings between you will be established.

There will always be issues requiring families and teachers to communicate with each other. But family needs affecting children in school are changing. Schools realize that to best meet children's learning needs they must reach out more than ever for your support and encourage you to increase your interaction with the school. Everyone must work together for each child's benefit.

In addition, research has shown that parental involvement positively affects children's success. To encourage families to participate in their children's education national, state, district, and local school efforts are establishing vehicles such as parent education programs, literacy programs, parent centers, and extended roles for PTOs through which families and schools can share, learn, and be involved together. Schools also continuously reach out to families for their assistance in addressing other critical elements in schools such as those associated with classroom issues, school budgets, school safety, or respect for human differences. This complex network is ultimately aimed at meeting children's needs. Achieving these goals in partnership with families requires home-school communication.

Opportunities for you to communicate with your child's school are vast. Communicating effectively with your child's teacher is one significant way you can contribute to helping your child progress. Become involved at a level where you feel comfortable. You could discover that if you are effective in communicating with your child's teacher, you will become confident in your skills and motivated to apply them to other home-school areas.

You and your child are continuously learning. As your child proceeds through school, you too will experience new challenges and opportunities. This book offers suggestions, but ultimately you must choose the route that is best for you.

Welcome chances to communicate with your child's teachers during the elementary school years as valuable experiences from which you and your child will benefit. Never again throughout your child's school career will the opportunities for exchange be quite the same.